Jesus
of Nazareth

12/23

D0383384

Jesus
of Nazareth

How He Understood His Life

Raymund Schwager

Translated by
James G. Williams

A Crossroad Book
The Crossroad Publishing Company
New York

1998

The Crossroad Publishing Company
370 Lexington Avenue, New York, NY 10017

Originally published as *Dem Netz des Jägers entronnen — Das Jesusdrama nacherzählt*,
copyright © 1991 by Kösel-Verlag GmbH & Co., Munich.

English translation and preface copyright © 1998 by James G. Williams

All rights reserved. No part of this book may be reproduced, stored in a re-
trieval system, or transmitted, in any form or by any means, electronic, mechan-
ical, photocopying, recording, or otherwise, without the written permission of
The Crossroad Publishing Company.

Printed in the United States of America

Library of Congress Cataloging-in-Publication Data
Schwager, Raymund.
    [Dem Netz des Jägers entronnen. English]
    Jesus of Nazareth : how he understood his life / Raymund Schwager ;
translated by James G. Williams.
        p.   cm.
    ISBN 1-8245-1711-3 (pbk.)
    1. Jesus Christ – Fiction.   I. Title.
PT2680.W25D46   1998
232.9'01–dc21   97-45152
                                                                      CIP

Contents

Translator's Preface

Is it possible to say how Jesus understood his life? To many lay readers of the Gospels the answer is obvious: Yes, of course; it's only necessary to read the New Testament Gospels. But in biblical scholarship the answer is not obvious at all. Indeed, it is now a commonplace in historical-critical exegesis — study of the Bible which draws out the text's meaning in terms of its historical background and context — that it is impossible to penetrate into Jesus' inner life and find out what he really thought about himself and his mission. In fact, the majority of critical scholars hold that the accounts of his resurrection, his acceptance of the role of Messiah, and the miracles he performed are all *fictions* which were created by the Christian tradition once the post-Jesus movement got underway.

One of the pioneers of modern New Testament criticism, Rudolf Bultmann, argued that one could not know anything about Jesus' personal awareness, although it was possible to infer important aspects of his "self-understanding." By self-understanding (*Selbstverständnis*) Bultmann meant what Jesus expressed and implied about himself in his public work — preaching of the kingdom of God, performing healings and exorcisms, associating with marginal and outcast people, etc. Raymund Schwager dares to mean much more than that in *Jesus of Nazareth: How He Understood His Life*.

Schwager's dare is simultaneously an intellectual risk and a venture of faith. Its point of departure is a theme of the great theological tradition of the church, and it is fleshed out through the inspiration of two great modern thinkers. The great theological tradition offers the principle of the fulfillment of Old Testament prophecies and covenants in Christ. Schwager has written a narrative showing Jesus in constant engagement with the faith of Israel. His way of understanding Jesus places him within a world of biblical texts. Jesus presupposes these texts, meditates on them, confronts them, and argues with them as he fulfills his mission from the Father. This is why all quotations from the Old Testament have been rendered in **bold type**; they are meant to stand out as the transmission of God's own voice from the past in Jesus' world. Jesus' own words are always, directly or indirectly, his response to the scriptural voice from the past and to his sense of the presence and guidance of the Father. They have been placed in *italics*.

The two thinkers who have so greatly influenced Schwager are Hans Urs von Balthasar and René Girard. Von Balthasar proposed *drama*, specifically a "God-drama," as the most meaningful way to do theology.[1] The perspective of drama enables Schwager both to realize the dramatic potential of the gospel story and to portray the freedom of Jesus to accept and shape his mission within the larger history of God.

René Girard, known for his analysis of the human condition which begins and ends with Jesus' passion and resurrection,[2] offers a convincing depiction of the complicity of all of us in the sort of structures based on collective violence that led to the crucifixion of Jesus. Schwager's understanding of rivalry, Jesus as model who imitates God the Father, and Jesus' freedom to forgive his enemies has been shaped by Girard's thought.

Schwager is convinced that portraying Jesus dramatically within his historical context and world of biblical references will result in a picture truer and more valuable than most of the scholarly investigations, which have wandered far afield from the life of authentic Christian faith. In fact, the author has written a complementary scholarly volume, *Jesus im Heilsdrama: Entwurf einer biblischen Erlösungslehre* (Jesus in the Drama of Salvation: Sketch of a Biblical Doctrine of

---

1. H. U. von Balthasar, *Theo-Drama*, 3 vols. so far published in English (San Francisco: Ignatius Press, 1988–96).

2. For a full view of his work, particularly in religion and theology, see R. Girard, *The Girard Reader*, ed. James G. Williams (New York: Crossroad, 1996).

Redemption). In it, he seeks to substantiate the present portrayal of Jesus through a systematic analysis of biblical research.

The author's way of unfolding the gospel drama of Jesus not only presents a coherent and meaningful picture of Jesus, his work and spirituality, but provides at the same time a rich introduction to the Old Testament as the church's book.

It has been a great joy for me to translate Father Schwager's narrative. May the reading of this book result in insight, discernment, and blessing for the reader.

JAMES G. WILLIAMS
July 21, 1997

Jesus
of Nazareth

Beginnings

Maturing in Stillness

A voice called his name loudly. Where did it come from? Who spoke to him? Had he dreamed it, or was someone actually calling him? He sat up in the darkness, listened, but could hear nothing more. He lay back down, and in the silence the voice that he had heard earlier came again (Ps. 81:5), and it was strangely familiar to him. When he once more could not detect anyone, a story came to him, the story of the young Samuel: Samuel had confused the voice of the Lord with that of a human when it first called to him. The priest Eli was clear-sighted and instructed the lad that he had to respond to the Lord (1 Sam. 3:1–10). With an alert and expectant heart Jesus lay down again. When the voice came to him for the third time it was like a whisper, and he answered in the darkness, *Speak, Lord, your servant hears.* At the same time he opened himself to the whispered sound that had reached his ear and his heart. His whole being was alive, and he drifted out of the everyday world. A figure who had the appearance of a man (Dan. 7:13) and was translucent like an angel emerged before him. The mysterious voice that had called him spoke now with words of comfort (Zech. 1:13) to this figure: **Son of Man, I am giving you to the house of Israel as a watchman and redeemer** (Ezek. 3:17). The words struck him and opened a space in his soul which he had never before passed through. Winged creatures appeared who praised the one calling to him as they sang and called out to each other, **Holy is the Lord of lords** (Isa. 6:1–4).

Jesus stood up, fell to his knees, and bowed deeply until his forehead touched the ground. He remained there for a long time. He allowed the newly opened space in his soul to become full of the praise the winged creatures were singing and calling out to each other. The figure like a human being came up close to him. Who was this? He felt deeply connected to it, yet at the same time it affected him like a great question. An odd mixture of deepest familiarity and great uncertainty stemmed from it. But he knew he had time and must wait, in spite of the call he experienced.

In the coming weeks and months his mind often went back to the voice that had sounded in his ear and fallen into his soul. Also the song of the winged creatures resounded still in him, and the more his soul joined in with it the more clearly he was convinced that everything he was experiencing had already been long familiar to him. Images out of early childhood became fresh once more, and out of the great sea of the past images arose which he had never suppressed, but which had easily sunk under the threshold of consciousness. When he didn't yet understand how to choose the good and reject the evil (Isa. 7:16), he had often felt himself strangely supported and held. He felt deeply the sense of security when he was taken into his mother's arms or spent time near her, and already at that age the sacred songs of Israel gripped him. Yet the more he matured, the stronger the power of the peace from the depths of his own heart radiated out to him. And now the figure accompanied him and led his steps like an angel.

With God and among Human Beings

He spent many hours outside the village in the solitude of nature. The great silence that lay like a protective space over the mountainous terrain received him. All things confronted him as if they could speak, and they imprinted themselves on his soul. In the spring he gave himself over to observing a lily or in hot dry summer to regarding a thistle. He saw as signs of the future stony and dusty roads which ran between the fields into the distance and disappeared behind the next hill. Birds flew over and sought their meager nourishment. He found nothing to be ordinary or everyday. All of nature spoke to him and tried to tell him something. Yet he did not understand what the strange words proceeding from all things had to say to him. He only heard how they softly sounded and praised their Creator.

The people in the village liked the son of Mary and the carpenter, but they considered him odd. His hands were skillful in the work with his father and intent on completing the work begun (Sir. 38:27). Still, however, he was no worker like others, for his heart searched out mysteries (Sir. 39:7). His friendliness radiated out to the neighbors and everyone in the village; yet he wasn't like other young people. Why was he alone so often? Why did he pose questions for which no one had an answer and which came across as very disconcerting out of the mouth of a young man? People talked about him a lot in his absence, and here and there jokes were made about him, but these soon faded away because no one could be mad at him and many were devoted to him. An air of fascination surrounded him.

As soon as he walked into their circles, their everyday way of talking changed. Even though there were no great matters to recount, still he wanted to hear what they did in their work, how things were going in their families, and what they got out of going to the synagogue. When Jesus began asking questions, many noticed that they had many experiences which they had forgotten, but which Jesus brought to mind. Tongues which were otherwise dumb or could only imitate the conversation and laughter of others found their speech in his presence. Some were able to feel only later how they had suddenly, through him, been able to speak and to recount much about their joys and sufferings. In his presence their own life became more intense, free, and cheerful. It began to strike them how their own talk was usually banal, yes, even rough and offensive. Although he never rebuked them, uneasy and self-critical thoughts began to stir up in them. So it was that people sought to be with him and yet at the same time avoided him. They could not understand him, and so many relieved their uneasiness with little jokes.

What he himself really thought, nobody knew. It caused something of a stir that already as a young boy he had learned to read and write and was often occupied with the Holy Scriptures. Yet contrary to expectations he was not a student of the learned scribes, and although he sought wisdom he did not attend any house of learning. He went his own way and was able, already at a young age, to embarrass even respected scribes. He seemed to be a student of the Torah, the five books of narrative and instruction that God gave to Israel through Moses. However, he did not become attached to the fellowship of the Pharisees, the experts in Torah who were very pious and pledged themselves to exact observance of the prescriptions for tithing and purity. He frequented those who had to work hard for their daily bread. So what would become of him?

Many Greek-speaking gentiles resided in nearby Sepphoris, and the Romans ruled in Jerusalem, the city of the Temple. Roman influence could also be felt in Galilee, although here Herod Antipas ruled. Herod was a foreign and cruel sovereign who was never able to win the heart of the people. (He was the son of that Herod who rebuilt the Temple with great brilliance.) The gentiles who now had the upper hand in the land of the elect did not believe in the God of the fathers and showed only contempt for the traditions. Why had God permitted such a heavy burden and great misfortune to come upon his people? Had they sinned so greatly, or were these troubles a sign of the distress and need that must precede the end of the old world and the beginning of the new time of salvation (Dan. 12:1–12)?

The people of Galilee talked about these questions continually, but their conversations always ended in perplexity. Everyone still had a lively recollection of Judas of Gamala, who inspired many among the people in the time of the great census and stirred them to resistance against the Romans. In flaming speeches he painted before the eyes of the young men the nearness of the time of salvation for which they had long yearned. It would have to be brought to pass through open battle, and the gentiles, who are exalted today, would disappear by tomorrow (1 Macc. 2:63). He praised the heroic deed of the priest Pinhas, who in ancient days was passionately zealous for Yahweh and ran his spear through an unfaithful Israelite in bed with his foreign woman. Thanks to this holy and bloody deed atonement was made for the entire people and a plague averted that had already made victims of many. The priest Pinhas and his descendants were granted a covenant of peace and an everlasting priesthood (Num. 25:6–13). Would God not act likewise today if the people began to show zeal for him?

Judas of Gamala also made the events in the period of the Maccabees spring up in shining colors before the eyes of the people. At that time a great crisis occurred in Israel because Jerusalem had been subjected to a blasphemous act. Pagans ruled in the land and had desecrated the Temple by bringing into it the abomination of an idol. But Mattathias and his sons did not merely complain about this source of misery (1 Macc. 2:6–13), as many of the pious did; they made themselves into the arm of the Lord. When an apostate from their own people defied them and began to offer blasphemous sacrifice before their eyes, they were seized with holy zeal and did what Pinhas had once done. They stabbed the unfaithful Israelite at the altar and slew the royal official who wanted to compel them to offer the pagan sacrifice. They fled into the mountains in order to gather there the true devotees of the holy Torah. With the help of God they were able to defend themselves against the troops of the foreign king who pursued them, and Judas, son of Mattathias, was enabled to win back the Jerusalem Temple and liberate Israel (1 Macc. 2:15–4:61).

> **He went through the cities of Judah,**
> **he destroyed the wicked in the land**
> **and turned God's wrath away from Israel.**
> **People spoke of him to the ends of the earth.**
>   (1 Macc. 3:8–9)

In his speeches Judas had ardently entreated God for assistance and acclaimed the past mighty acts that occurred thanks to the arm of the Lord. Yet his fate was different from that of Pinhas and Mattathias. He was able neither to ward off the plague nor to drive out the Romans. He could not bring about the longed for kingdom of God, for he himself and many of his followers fell in battle, while the others scattered. Since then many spoke of him openly in Galilee as a false prophet who had misled the people. However, in the hearts of others he still lived and inspired dreams full of holy zeal.

Wrestling with Scripture

People often asked Jesus son of the carpenter how he viewed Judas
of Gamala and when the Messiah would come. Yet he never gave
a clear answer. He always emphasized, to be sure, that the decision of the Lord could not be forced (Jud. 8:16). But at the same
time he liked to pose confusing counterquestions: Where now is
the everlasting priesthood after the order of Pinhas, since yet others
were meanwhile installed as high priests (1 Macc. 10:15–21)? Why
are the Romans now in the land if the Maccabees liberated and
purified it of all pagans? No one could answer these and similar questions, and so finally most of them avoided bringing them up with
him again.

The questions he directed to others followed his own quest, which
took him further day by day. He thought about the years long past
(Ps. 77:6), and the promise of the land, which had driven many of
his brothers in the faith in their holy zeal, preoccupied him also. How
often had he read, and heard in sermons, that God had promised the
land of Canaan to the ancestors Abraham, Isaac, and Jacob (Gen.
13:14–16). How often had he been told, from earliest childhood on,
the story of how the Lord freed his people with a mighty hand from
Egypt, the house of bondage, and led them through the wilderness
into the promised land. With special fascination and inner stirrings
he himself had read those words over and over that were given to the
people through Moses on the other side of the Jordan. These were
words full of promise (Deut. 8:7–9:8).

Yet what would come of these words? The people had lived where
the Lord wanted to lead them, of course, since the time of Joshua.
They were, however, no longer the masters of their own land. Pagans ruled over Israel, and instead of the promised blessing there
was everywhere illness, poverty, and need. Was this a punishment
from God, as Moses had already announced (Deut. 29:15–30:10)
and as had already broken out once on the people when the Babylonian troops had conquered Jerusalem, destroyed the Temple, and
taken away the survivors to a distant captivity? But this punishment

in the time of the prophet Jeremiah finally came to an end. After many years the people could return to Jerusalem under the rule of the Persian king Cyrus, whom God had chosen as his instrument. However, this return to the homeland was not as wonderful and glorious as the prophets had proclaimed (Jer. 30:18–31:14). The foreign rule continued on and life in the land God had given was meager and wearying — so completely different than declared in the ancient promises (Deut. 30:1–10).

Even the attempt of the Maccabees to drive out the godless rulers brought no real improvement. Could the unfaithfulness and stiff-necked character of the people (Ps. 78:17, 40, 56) delay the plans of God and postpone the fulfillment of the promises indefinitely? Could they really be any better if even Moses had been drawn into denial and failure through the murmuring of the people (Num. 20:1–13)? Indeed, the prophets had prophesied both a transformation of the hearts that had become stone and a new covenant (Jer. 31:33); but many centuries had passed by since then. When would the words of promise became reality?

With all these questions Jesus was so drawn to his God in his heart that he rose up completely into the reality of **I am the Lord** (Isa. 43:11). Was the day about to come that his people had so long awaited? For the time being the question remained open for him as to where the figure, the form that appeared to him, the guardian and redeemer of Israel, would lead him. Everything to come he gave over to his God, into whose presence he prayerfully plunged as into a great sea.

He went regularly to the synagogue on the Sabbath. The rejoicing and thanksgiving of the praying community (Ps. 42:5) lent him solidarity with the people of his neighborhood. Yet the Scripture readings and sermons also posed new questions for him. He heard often from the Books of Moses about what was clean and unclean. All animals which have divided hoofs, cloven feet, and chew the cud may be eaten, but the others may not be (Lev. 11:3–4). The preachers clarified in detail which of the known animals were to be numbered among the clean animals and which among the unclean. Jesus wondered why God, who tested hearts (Ps. 17:3), should also give attention to divided hoofs, cloven feet, and chewing the cud. He could find no reason why this eating should make one's heart unclean. Thinking about this brought to his mind in clearer relief scenes in which people attacked one another, spread suspicions around, and carried on with angry words. Everyone seemed to find pleasure in disparaging others. Was this not the true breeding place of so much evil? But the synagogue preachers scarcely touched on this, preferring to speak of animals, of tithes, sacrifices, and laws. After the worship service they mixed outside the synagogue with that very crowd in which people laughed about those not present, and soon suspicions and angry words were flying around. Weren't these words like poisonous arrows (Ps. 64:4)? The less Jesus understood about the cleanness and uncleanness of animals, the more he saw the careless tongues as like a warrior's sharp arrows (Ps. 120:4). He felt like an alien who was in distant Meshech and must dwell in the dark tents of Kedar (Song 1:5), with the hostile and violent people of the east (Jer. 49:28), while he longed to dwell in the tents of the upright (Ps. 118:5).

When the Books of Moses were read he was quite taken aback by the instructions to remove transgressors of the Torah from the people and to punish them with death. Would not almost the entire people have to be eradicated if this kind of ordinance were completely upheld? He couldn't remember whether anyone had ever been stoned because of offense against the Torah. Of course, the story was told that Judas of Gamala had ordered Torah breakers to be executed during his rebellion against the Romans. But had the rebels really acted out of zeal for God's command, or were they rather addicted to the zeal for power?

On the great festival days he made the pilgrimage with the people from Galilee up to Jerusalem, as the Torah prescribed (Deut. 16:16). A great bustle of traffic constantly prevailed there. Although he rejoiced that he could make pilgrimage to the house of the Lord (Ps. 122), he never experienced there the peace that he so cherished in solitude outside the villages of Galilee. And then in the Temple! He longed to be able to spend his time in a chamber of prayer (Ps. 27:4). Yet the

noise and pushing of crowds that prevailed in the holy place! The ped-
dlers of sacrificial animals cried out, and the masses pushed their way
into the galleries and the forecourt of the Temple, while the animals
themselves were restless and spread about them a stench which was
no pleasing aroma to rise up to the Lord (Sir. 35:8). What affected
him and gave him greatest pause for reflection were the sacrifices,
which were offered just as the Torah prescribed: the daily morning
and evening sacrifice, the offerings of first fruits at the time of the
harvest, and the many young bulls, rams, lambs, and billy goats on
the festival days (Num. 29:12–39). All this happened — according to
the words of Moses — to make a pleasant fragrance for the Lord
(Num. 15:3, 10, 13). But did God actually have joy in this bloody
business?

He himself often stood in the crowd of pilgrims when the animals
were killed. He saw how the blood flowed and was sprinkled on the
altar. He smelled the incense, the flowing blood and burnt flesh, and
this smell was repulsive to him. At such times he identified himself
again with the words of the prophets against sacrifices:

> I hate your feasts, I despise them,
> and I cannot stand your solemn festivals.
> I take no pleasure in your burnt offerings
>   and cereal offerings,
> I will not accept them,
> and the peace offerings of your fatted beasts
>   I will not regard. (Amos 5:21–22)

As the white knife sliced into the bodies of the sacrificial animals
and the blood gushed out, Jesus observed the people who stood around
him. He saw and felt an excitement which repelled him. Even the
priests slaughtered the creatures as if they had no inkling of what
they did as they were cutting with the knife. It was as though they
were motivated by strange powers and addicted to a secret intoxication
for blood. The blood of the victim that stuck to their hands was like
the blood of humans (Isa. 1:15). At such festivals Jesus could not find

that peace which is inner blessedness. The cloud of smoke from the sacrifices that enwrapped the Temple was certainly no pleasing odor to the Lord.

Did the many rituals, at least through the faithfulness of their execution, promote obedience and reverence for the God of the covenant? He hesitated in reflection, and then he gladly recalled an oracle of Jeremiah which came to expression from his heart:

I did not speak to your fathers when I led them out of Egypt, nor did I command them, concerning burnt offerings and sacrifices. (Jer. 7:22)

Could it be that the sacrifices don't really go back to an ordinance from God and are a human invention (Amos 5:25)? But in the Books of Moses just to the contrary was stated. They reported exactly how God commanded the many sacrifices and had warned the people against removing any of the instructions or adding any new ones (Deut. 11:1, 8). Jesus was clear in his own mind that many passages of Scripture were obscure. Only through giving oneself over to the Spirit of the Lord might one hope to understand correctly the words of Moses and the prophets.

At the festival liturgy in the Temple trumpets sounded which were played by the priests. The Levites played on cymbals, harps, and zithers (2 Chron. 5:12), and they sang the holy songs of Israel while the people fell to the ground, so that the sweet melody of jubilation resounded (Sir. 50:18). Although the sacrifices disturbed him, his soul could completely soar in the resounding drums and clanging cymbals to honor that God who made an end to death and war (Jud. 16:1–2). Yet the song of praise (Ps. 150) didn't last very long, and most of the pilgrims who lingered in the Temple seemed to be more moved by the sacrifices than by the common prayer. So at that point he gladly returned to Galilee.

His home village was built on cliffs, and also the cliffs of nearby mountains looked over toward it. He loved to walk over the immovable stones and so listen to words which gave his steps a foothold:

> He set my feet upon the rock,
> making my steps secure.
> He put a new song in my mouth,
> a song of praise to him, our God.
>   (Ps. 40:2b–3a)

When he was alone he liked to sing, and he constantly heard — deeply in his ear and outside in everything — a delicate humming and soft, high ringing, like many cicadas giving a concert on a warm summer night or the stars lightly playing in the way through the sky (Sir. 43:9). Also the form of the Son of Man did not leave him since it appeared to him for the first time. Of course, he seldom perceived it with his bodily eyes, but he felt it with his inner senses, how it accompanied him in all his ways (Ps. 91:11).

Often he remembered an evening hour outside close to the village. A great dark storm cloud had drawn up in the sky. (Or had it arisen within him?) Nightfall came, and in the darkness he saw suddenly a fire (Deut. 4:11–12) and a flaming torch (Gen. 15:17) which moved back and forth. The red light came up to him as if it would confront him eye to eye (Exod. 33:11). He held his breath. But then the approaching red light, which now took on the features of a royal countenance (Ps. 47:3), turned to the form of the Son of Man beside him. He was overcome with a deep shudder and could see nothing more (Deut. 4:12). Yet right away his breath returned again and he felt the rock on which his feet stood (Ps. 40:3). A hand protected him as in the cleft of a rock, while the ineffable power and glory passed by (Exod. 33:7–23). He heard a whisper (Job 28:22) and sensed a consuming strength and might.

The people were in dread at Mt. Sinai when Yahweh revealed himself in thunder and lightning, with the sound of horns and in smoke from the mountain. They sent Moses before them because they thought they would surely die in a direct encounter with the God of the covenant (Exod. 20:18–20). Then the Tent of Meeting was likewise so holy that only the Levites dared approach it without being struck dead (Num. 1:51), and the holy things had to be hidden even

from their eyes (Num. 4:17–20). The most frightening thing, however, was the Holy of Holies. Even the high priest had to fill and
screen it with the smoke of incense when he was annually obliged
to enter it with the blood of the atonement, so that the consuming
holiness of God would not break out with a deadly curse over the
land of the covenant people (Lev. 16). Jesus often wondered what this
dangerous holiness could really mean. Even though his soul shook
too when it drew close to its God, he nevertheless felt no anxiety,
and he never feared that he would be slain. Had the consuming holiness of God not been yet illuminated for him, or was the God of
Israel showing himself to him in a manner which surpassed everything else in the history of his people? He trusted completely what
he felt with unshakable certainty, and entrusted the open questions to
the future.

The Time of Marriage

The years passed. Jesus' friends of his own age had all married, and
in the village people thought it was about time for him also to give
Israel new sons and daughters. People whispered about who his choice
of bride would be. Among the women who met by the spring, in
the field, or in the evening, there were always new speculations. His
mother Mary was asked. Yet she seemed herself to know nothing of
the plans of her son, and she replied that he would do the right thing
when the time came. If anyone asked him directly, he just smiled and
said he was still waiting for his bride. Yet when he said this his words
sounded so strange that many wondered whether he was thinking of
a specific young woman at all.

He enjoyed reading of love in the Song of Songs. He was astonished how the yearning between the king's son and the girl cast a spell
over the entire world and how their love seemed to float over mead-
ows, gardens, and vineyards. It transformed the streets and squares
of the city, rested on hills of incense and mountains of myrrh, and
longed for the spring after the cold winter. In this song had wise King

Solomon only composed a momentary dream with beautiful words? Jesus had known already some lads from the village who spoke with drunken enthusiasm of their first love of girls. However, some years later they sang a completely different tune. The bride so extolled soon became the scolding wife in the house they shared (Prov. 21:9). What was love all about? Was it only a beautiful nighttime dream, which must soon live in the sober light of morning, or was it a mysterious power which changes the whole world?

> **Strong like death is love,**
> **passion is cruel as the grave.**
> **Its flashes are flashes of fire,**
> **powerful, powerful flames.**
> (Song 8:6)

These words echoed in his ears and he believed them, although he had still until now not encountered such a love among humans. Did not the Wisdom of God call out in similar fashion in all the streets of the city and at all the crossroads of the land (Prov. 8:2)? Whatever drew him to his God, he experienced it as powerful flames and embers of fire. He believed quite as a matter of course that the passion of his heart was stronger than the underworld and was able to change the entire world. But what was the place of human love in this? He knew, for the time being, no conclusive answer, and so he kept the images of the song like a closed garden and a sealed-off fountain in his heart (Song 4:12).

The people of his village saw that he let the time of marriage pass by. Some said that they had never expected otherwise of him. Wouldn't he be more suited for that community which lived by the Dead Sea and whose members led an austere life and never married? Strange things were told of these people. Why did they separate from others and go out into the wilderness? Why did they practice so many rituals and yet did not go up to Jerusalem on the festival days, as the Torah prescribed (Exod. 34:23)? This strange community aroused mistrust in many, while others were amazed at their zeal for purity.

Still others said Jesus would never go there. He was, they opined, very pious, but he still didn't take the Torah seriously enough. He went around with people from whom a faithful adherent of the Torah would do better to keep his distance, and he conversed alone with women, which was not proper. Especially James, a pious man and one of his close relatives, did not understand why his brother showed no great zeal for the instructions given by Moses.

Jesus liked to spend time among the simple folk who understood little of the Torah. Among them he often heard how worried they were about children, relatives, or neighbors. He found in some of them a great readiness to take pains and make sacrifices, and he felt sometimes a love which touched him. Even here, however, he had experiences which did not allow him to feel at home. The poor people too were hardly different in their speech and judgments from the learned in the Torah. They also could easily attack with sharp words those weak and absent. He did not want ever to sit in the circle of the scoffers (Ps. 1:1), and he detested catching a brother or a sister in a net of suspicions (Ps. 35:7).

He was close to his fellow humans and yet at the same time distant and foreign (Ps. 69:8). How could he help them understand what moved him when he himself could scarcely find the right words for it? A gentle power often flowed into his soul without reaching a bottom. The more he drank of it, the more he thirsted. Then again it was as if he lost the ground under his feet, fell out into a broad and open space, and then was borne up by hands (Ps. 91:12). When he answered the call **Seek my face,** from the depth of his heart (Ps. 27:8), he became fused with this call, so that his answer became a new call. He was well informed in images and dreams (Dan. 1:17), but he let himself be guided completely by the form that accompanied him. One day he thought he was able to determine, to his great surprise, that it followed him and was becoming more and more like him. He could not find anything comparable even among the prophets.

Consecrated in His Mother's Womb

The clearer it became to him that he had to go entirely his own way, images from the past were even more powerful — images from the distant past arising in his soul. Once he had an experience as if he were in a dark space, his body hidden in warm waters (Ps. 104:6) and enclosed by distant oscillations and sounds. His memory, which reached far back, remained fixed on words known to him:

Before I formed you in the womb I knew you,
and before you were born I consecrated you.

(Jer. 1:5)

These words made something vibrate in his heart which he could not grasp, and he let the question of how God would have consecrated him in his mother's womb sink into himself. He opened his soul to the images that rose up and were held in suspense within him. Then he resolved to ask his mother at an opportune moment what she had experienced as she carried him in her womb.

The right moment came soon, and it turned out differently from what he had expected. His mother seemed at first embarrassed by his question. She was silent for a long time. Then she began to recount from the holy books how barren women, after long waiting, had conceived a child by the grace of the Lord. She spoke as if she intended to evade his question. Finally she looked at him, lowered then her gaze, and began to speak softly in a way she had never done before. Word after word flew to him and touched his soul. Soon she stopped talking, and then both of them sat there for a long time in silence. After he had wordlessly stood up and gone out, he left the village. The account of the work of God in his mother's womb had taken on an unexpected meaning for him, and his Father in heaven came even closer to him. But still he didn't understand what the secret of his origin was saying to him. However, there was greater clarity that a mission to his people awaited him. For the moment he gave himself over to a meditation of thanksgiving.

Everything that he heard from the Holy Scriptures and that he
himself read came into the light of the one great holy word:

**Hear, O Israel! The Lord is our God, the Lord is one. There-
fore you shall love the Lord your God with your whole heart,
your entire soul, and with all your might.** (Deut. 6:4)

To Jesus this love did not involve should and must. It was the secret
of his soul, a sweet gift, and there were many hours that it intoxicated
him. While a light shudder would make his skin tingle, a tender desire
arose from the depth of his body, filled his heart, and penetrated his
spirit, and then, as in a whisper, stream to that one, the form of the
Son of Man, who was so close to him. He had no word for what
passed through him, for all signs and images of the Scriptures didn't
seem adequate for expressing it. But he held even more to the form
that accompanied him like a second self. He followed it, and it came
closer to him.

Presentiment of Things to Come

He felt no inner fire for God among the preachers in the synagogue
and only seldom a real enthusiasm for the knowledge of God (Hos.
4:1). They were zealous about trivialities of the Torah, but this zeal
did not affect him and indeed he found it troublesome. But he discovered he had to take into account that the authority of the scribes
and Pharisees was great among the common folk. Their knowledge of
the Holy Scriptures and especially their allusions to secret lore about
the ways of God conferred on them high esteem, which they knew
how to use to give themselves an aura of loftiness. People said that
only in the most intimate circle of students would they take up the
teachings concerning the sacred throne chariot vision (Ezek. 1:4–28),
the heavenly and subterranean worlds, and the last things. The simple people thus held them in great honor, which was often greater

than the respect they paid to the priests, as Jesus confirmed in his pilgrimages to Jerusalem.

Since he was sensing quite clearly the mission that awaited him, he often wondered how the scribes would react to him. He had not attended a school and could support himself only on his own inner certainty. Would they listen to what God gave him so clearly to know? And how would the priests react to him? He had often perceived what an impression the form of the high priest made when he appeared before the people in the great festivals in the splendor of his vestments (Exod. 28), which during the year were kept in security by the pagan Romans. His turban was adorned with a gold crown and bells hung on the hem of his garments announced his coming. On his shoulders he wore two carnelians in which the names of the twelve tribes of Israel had been inscribed, and on his breast was the ephod with twelve precious stones which likewise bore the names of the sons of Israel (Sir. 45:9–12). When he appeared in the magnificence of these vestments and surrounded by priests, he appeared to the people

> like a morning star among the clouds,
> like the full moon in the festival days,
> like the son shining on the Temple of the Most High,
> like a rainbow gleaming in the clouds,
> like branches of flowers in the festival days.
>
> (Sir. 50:6–8)

Would this morning star give heed to him? Jesus was more concerned about Yom Kippur, the Day of Atonement, than the high priest's attitude toward it. Yom Kippur was when the great rite of reconciliation was completed. On this day the high priest was required first to sacrifice a young bull for his own sins. Then the lot was cast over the two he-goats, one of which was determined for the Lord and the other for Azazel. The high priest carried the blood of the goat which was to be for a ransom to the Lord, together with coals and incense, into the Holy of Holies and sprinkled it on the mercy seat of the ark of the covenant for the people's atonement. Some of the blood he also

sprinkled on the altar in the inner forecourt of the Temple. After that
he laid his hands on the head of the second goat and in the name of
all the tribes of Israel, which were inscribed in the precious stones on
his garments, he placed the sins of all Israel on the animal. It would
then be immediately driven out of the Temple and the city into the
wilderness. Year by year Jesus had followed this great ritual, in which
the high priest was even permitted to speak the forbidden name of
God (Sir. 50:20), and he became profoundly certain that Israel could
not be truly redeemed and made holy by the blood of the one goat
and the ritual gestures over the other one. The ritual certainly brought
everyone's sins to mind, but they were too deep and resistant to be
taken away by a goat. What was needed was a pure water coming
from God to wash hearts clean (Ezek. 36:25); yes, a reconciliation
was necessary which would bring a true peace into the life of human
beings with one another.

Once Jesus deliberately remained outside the Temple in order to
experience at first hand how the goat bearing the people's sins was
driven by the shouting of the crowd of pilgrims through the narrow
streets and out of the city. The sight of the frightened, driven animal and the wild cries of the crowd, which was beside itself, affected
him deeply, and for a moment he had the presentiment that a similar
fate could befall him some day. Therefore he visited the tombs of the
prophets that were located close to the city. The messengers of God
had proclaimed the words that came to them; for that they were often
persecuted by their own people.

Jesus loved to observe what the festival pilgrims did. He posed
questions to many of them, but they were scarcely understood by most
of them. This is how he made the acquaintance of two sisters who
resided in nearby Bethany with their brother. They were drawn to
the calmness and power that radiated from him, and soon they began
asking him questions in their own turn. He referred them continually
to the holy books. Yet they strongly felt that he read and interpreted
Scripture quite differently from the scribes. Their searching hearts intuited a peace in him which they had never found in the course of the
festival activities. On his part, he was able to express in their conver-

sations something of what had preoccupied him within and for which he had, until now, found so little understanding. So began a friendship which allowed him to begin to speak about what his coming mission might be. So he was pleased to be a frequent guest in Bethany as often as he made the pilgrimage to Jerusalem.

First Act

Calling to the Wonder of God's Rule

As John was preaching at the Jordan a hot wind broke loose from the heights in the wilderness and a storm cloud drew near (Jer. 4:11, 13). Misfortune and great destruction threatened from the north (Jer. 6:1). In the storm that sprang up the raging of the peoples could be heard (Ps. 2:1). The words of the Baptizer were like whiplashes, and it was as if the prophet Elijah had called down fire from heaven on all godlessness (1 Kings 18:20–40). His haggard form and his clothing were a testimony to the seriousness of his words. They affected all hearers, and more and more people streamed to him from Jerusalem, Judea, and the entire region of the Jordan.

The preaching allowed nobody to escape. It was different from the preaching in the synagogues by the teachers of the Torah, who for the most part slipped into a tone which betrayed their contempt for the simple folk and those unversed in the Torah. John thundered at these very scribes and Pharisees: "You brood of vipers, do you think you will be able to escape the coming judgment?" The preacher knew that those addressed justified themselves in their own minds against the indictment and appealed to that covenant which Yahweh had concluded with Abraham and his descendants (Gen. 15:1–21). Yet John did not allow even the original promise to Israel to count as a sign of hope: "You deceive yourselves when you appeal to Abraham as your father. His true descendants are not according to the flesh. I tell you, God is able to raise up true children to Abraham even from these stones." The preacher would grant only one valid response: repentance. As a sign of true penitence he demanded that the hearers be baptized, so that they could be redeemed in the imminent storm of judgment.

The Voice of the Father and the Mask of the Tempter

Jesus mingled among those who listened to John. What he heard moved and excited him. The message of the Baptizer, that God would soon appear in might and intervene in the destiny of his people, corresponded to what had occurred to him more and more clearly in recent years. Was this the sign for which he had waited so long? Finally he had met a son of Israel who was completely gripped by the God of the covenant and who openly named for what it was the dark world in whose spell the people lived. And yet... the preacher proclaimed the God who has come near in almost the same dark colors with which he denounced the evil prevailing among human beings. Was the Lord of Israel really so threatening? In no way did that match his previous experience. Of course, there were times when his happiness appeared to him like a deep abyss and he could not make out what yet lay hidden in its depths. Did God perhaps have a dark side in which he appeared as menacing to sinners? The question of God's wrath rose suddenly in him with new force. The violent shaking coming from the preacher ran through the crowd; he could feel its vibration deep within himself. His soul thirsted for clarity, and so he approached the Baptizer. He was convinced that only from the impending action of God that John announced could he hope for clarification of what was still enigmatic in Scripture and what he bore in himself as an unfathomable secret.

He got into the long line of those ready to be baptized. There were people in front of him and he was aware of others who pressed in behind him. He felt their breath and he smelled the sweat of the crowd. Pressing, panting, groaning — how much suffering and yearning, yet also how much harshness and evil were in these bodies? Jesus sensed with all the pores of his body how he had been unexpectedly drawn into a world which had not touched him before. What was happening to him? When it was his turn, the Baptizer was startled and stepped back a little. He looked with astonishment at the man who stood before him and was struck by something in his appearance (1 Sam. 10:23). He wanted to stop baptizing, but Jesus compelled him to continue. Hesitatingly John relented, and while the Baptizer placed his hand on him Jesus climbed into the water.

As he submerged he began to experience a shaking which seemed to make the foundations of the earth sway (Ps. 18:8). He felt as though the ground under his feet was losing its solidity. He climbed quickly back out of the water, but the shaking continued. The landscape, the nearby mountains, the whole world and the firmament above became alive. Light penetrated his spirit and his consciousness was extended until it merged with the landscape that surrounded him. Then the sky opened over him. Something like the gentle brush of a wing touched him and an infinitely delicate breath wafted about him. It touched his body and sank into his soul (Gen. 2:7) without reaching bottom or barrier. Jesus no longer knew where he stood and felt as though he was being borne up. He didn't lose consciousness, but it was as though a strange and yet familiar spirit that embraced the whole of things was breathing through him. Out of the open expanse came forth a voice (Num. 7:89), and he heard with great clarity: **This is my beloved son, with whom I am well pleased.** The words referred to the form of the Son of Man who constantly accompanied him, and yet they were directed to him. They penetrated to his very marrow. Suddenly it flashed to him: *The form was himself.* To a depth which remained a mystery to him he merged with the form even as he felt it beside him. Even though his consciousness still seemed to melt into infinity, yet everything happening was gathered together in the certainty that he himself was the beloved son. His feet felt once more the solid ground.

Nothing held him any longer in the crowd. He pushed his way out, in fact a force drove him away from people. He needed solitude in order to entrust himself both to the God who spoke to him and to the new self he had received. Everything ordinarily of importance in human life fell away from him. He didn't even think about eating. The wilderness received him like a great sheltering expanse and accompanied him in its profound silence.

All day what happened when he was with the Baptizer echoed within him. The blue firmament over the open wilderness gave a sense of reality to the image of the open heaven, and the drifting sand in the wind kept the experience of shaking alive in him. Since he could no longer find in the Holy Scriptures an image or form in which he recognized himself, he attached himself heart and soul to the word about the beloved son. He avoided examining more closely what it meant. While the air movement of the dove's beating wings enveloped him further (Song 6:9), he sensed a mysterious force which promised to guide him on the way that stretched ahead. And as he felt the gentle breath that had gone through him, images from the Song of Songs came to mind which he had borne for many years like a closed garden within himself:

> My dove in the clefts of the rock,
> hidden in the covert of the cliff,
> let me see your face,
> hear your voice!
> For your voice is sweet
> and lovely your face. (Song 2:14)

He felt himself as like a dove, like a bride whose heart awoke under the breath of the bridegroom, and he became aware of how God was inclined fully toward him. The words of the prophet Isaiah mounted in his heart:

> As the young man marries a maiden,
> so your builder marries you.
> As the bridegroom rejoices over the bride,
> so your God rejoices over you. (Isa. 62:5)

Suddenly he knew — these words also were spoken to him. He shook for happiness as first the voice of the dove and then the image from the prophet Isaiah appeared in the foreground of his consciousness. In the depths of his heart voice and image danced together and became united in a secret covenant. Yet they continued to be clearly distinct. The image of the bride loved by the bridegroom immediately quickened his human feeling and sensing. On the other hand, the word about the beloved son penetrated his spirit, his heart, and his body so deeply and so subtly that it could not be fastened down anywhere within him. He felt as if it was slipping away from him. But with the harmony of word and image he was filled with a peace deep as the sea. That power which addressed him from the height of heaven and the invisible depth of his heart was his loving Father. The word that the little children in Galilee used so confidently when they called to their fathers came involuntarily to his lips: *Abba.* He had to give thanks, and he gave thanks for a steadfast love which endures forever (Ps. 136:26).

The wilderness was devoid of humans. During the day a glaze of heat covered the sand and rocks, and by night it became painfully cold. He quenched his thirst at a small spring between the rocks whose water only some flowers and bushes and a solitary pine drank (Ps. 92:13). He wandered many hours there in inward conversation with his Abba, and there the gentle voice that he heard led his feet (Ps. 119:105) and enabled him to feel securely every stone. In the evening he would lie down with his back in the warm sand and observe the broad sky over him and the sudden appearance of the stars in their beauty and splendor (Sir. 43:9). For sleeping he took himself back near the spring into a cave (1 Kings 19:9) which had retained some of the heat of the day.

One evening a powerful storm came up. Black clouds clustered together (Sir. 43:15) and it became dark. Then the whole sky lighted up in the distance and a rumble could be heard. The lightning and fire in the sky came nearer. A wind came up and quickly grew to a storm and swept over the wilderness. Jesus went out into the open plain and walked with raised head against the storm. Darkness enveloped him and fire from heaven blazed about him; the thunder roared and even the rocks seemed to shake (Exod. 20:18). The whole of nature was in movement. The clouds poured out their water (Ps. 77:18), and the voice of the Lord sounded with power (Ps. 18:14). Yet the more powerfully the wilderness shook, so much more peace grew within him. He heard the mighty roaring, but at the same time it was like a gentle whisper (Job 4:16). His ears were opened wide, and as soon as thunder clapped he listened with great intensity to the subsequent stillness. His eyes were fixed far into the distance, and when lightning tore through the clouds, the splendor of the Lord radiated upon them (Ps. 18:13). His Abba approached him with powerful signs.

The storm faded away as suddenly as it had come. In the last rays of sun that soon broke through again a rainbow shone in resplendence (Gen. 9:12), and a soft light whisper (1 Kings 19:12) went through the wilderness. Jesus crouched down, touching his forehead to the ground, and the hand of the Lord came upon him once more (1 Kings 18:42, 46). After a long time he stood up. Meanwhile, the stars were shining in the sky, and the outlines of the nearby mountains appeared in the faded light. With head held high he stepped back into the night, and slowly he sorted out his thoughts about what had happened to him. He had heard the voice of his Abba in nature that had called to him in the baptism. All things had been drawn together in the covenant that he felt deep in his heart:

> **I will make for you a covenant on that day**
> **with the wild animals and the birds of the air,**
> **and with everything which creeps on the ground.**
> (Hos. 2:18)

The ancient promise of the land, which had preoccupied him so often, now became suddenly clear to him. In the thunderstorm he had experienced the powerful voice of the Lord as the presence of his Abba that made it possible for everything existing on the earth to become signs and parables. If he had earlier only felt how all things praised their Creator, now they began to speak to him of the Father. He knew they would help him bear his new message to others. His Father was King and Lord over all (Ps. 145:11–12). Overnight the rain had brought about a small miracle. Everything was budding and sprouting (Isa. 55:10), and the arid wilderness began to bloom like a garden (Isa. 32:15), while from its springs fresh water flowed out into the plain (Isa. 35:6). The bloom of a garden of paradise covered the dry wilderness ground for some hours, a sign of the rule of his Father.

In the ensuing days he spent much time listening anew to every thing in his surroundings. He could lose himself in the sight of thistles and stones in the wilderness or of flowers and bushes by his spring. He saw how the clouds and birds of the sky came by there, and everything spoke to him of the rule of his Father. He felt that he was accompanied with every step. All about him was a joyful singing (Ps. 65:13), and the lonely area became even more alive. He prayed, sang to himself the psalms of his people, and joined in the rejoicing that he discerned in the wilderness (Isa. 40:3). Sometimes he climbed up a mountain in the vicinity, from which he could look out over the greater part of the wilderness. There were mountains, hills, and narrow ravines. Farther away could be seen even the broad valley and the river in which he had been baptized.

> Why is it, O sea, that you flee,
> O Jordan, that you turn back?
> O mountains, that you skip like rams,
> O hills, like lambs? (Ps. 114:5–6)

The days passed quickly, and he became somewhat thinner. One morning he suddenly felt hungry again. A disturbing element had invaded his tremendous peace. He tried to pay no attention to it. But against his will the question arose within him: would his Abba feed him with manna as he had nourished the people in the wilderness? In his wandering about he took notice especially of the stones that as usual he allowed himself to feel, and he also continued to hold fast within himself to the word about the beloved son. Yet today the former blissful freedom was not present. The word did not ring fully in his soul, indeed it seemed even to become separated from him and independent, while everything remained mute and dark. He felt hunger once more. He wanted to divert himself and he deliberately regarded the stones in the hope of experiencing them as lucid signs from his Abba. Then suddenly everything crystalized: the word of the Father that had detached itself from him, the hunger he felt, and the stones that today remained lifeless. Very clearly he heard beside him, "If you are really the beloved son, then command that these stones become bread." He started and knew in the same moment that this was the sound of the tempter. He thought in a flash back to the great ordeal in the wilderness where God had allowed his people to go hungry so that they would not take the miraculous food for granted. Moses had drawn from the time of testing this teaching for Israel:

He wanted to make you understand that man does not live by bread alone, but by every word that comes from the mouth of the Lord. (Deut. 8:3)

Loud and decisively he repeated the words of Moses, and as soon as he spoke, the darkness that had gathered around him dissolved as if by itself. He felt himself to be free again.

He decided to climb up the mountain nearby so that he could praise his Abba along with the entire world that lay before him (Isa. 55:12) and to give thanks for the expulsion of the tempter. But while climbing he quickly became tired. Even before he reached the peak, everything became dark before his eyes. Was it his great fatigue, or was a storm moving in again as before when he was allowed to hear the voice of his Father in the trembling of nature? He remembered with what confidence he had set out that evening in the storm. But he soon perceived that this darkness was different. It was oppressive and he felt a great burden on himself, while the singing that accompanied him fell silent. Could he still find the peak of the mountain? Where was he anyway? Then a dark red fire tore through the darkness, glowing coals spewed out, and he heard thundering and blowing (Ps. 18:9–14). For just a moment the whole area could be seen in the dark glowing — indeed, the deeps of the sea and foundations of the earth were laid bare (Ps. 18:16). The whole world stretched out before him in this dark redness. The glowing coals looked as though they wanted to pull him into them. Everything started to get blurry before his eyes, and it seemed to him that he only had to give himself over to the undertow and he would be merged into everything. The entire dark world drew him, promised him everything. But deep in his heart the marvelous peace remained without breaking. And he knew suddenly — it was the tempter again. He closed his eyes, crouched down, and listened only to the peace within him. He felt the nearness of his Abba, and in worship he gave himself over only to him.

After a long time he stood up. The darkness and the eyes like glowing coals had vanished. The area again lay in peace before him, and he felt anew the singing that accompanied him. Of course he was still tired, but his soul was free and he could join wholeheartedly in the praise that goes throughout the world without words and without speech (Ps. 19:4). On the way back to the spring a question began to occupy him intensely. What was the tempter up to? Both times he had appeared to him under signs by which God made himself known to humans. The first time he concealed himself behind the stones and the word about the beloved son, while the second time he approached him almost under the cover of the same lights and callings of nature as his Abba previously had done (Ps. 18). Was it the tempter's very nature only to darken and twist God's own signs? Could his dark power even distort Scripture?

He had cherished a certain text since he couldn't remember when, yet at the same time he had been unable to understand it. The wise King Solomon said of that night in which God liberated his people from Egypt:

> For while deep silence enveloped all things
> and night in its course was half gone,
> your all-powerful word leaped from heaven
> as a stern warrior into the midst of the land devoted to
>   destruction.
> It carried the sharp sword of your inexorable command,
> it treaded along and filled all things with death;
> it touched the sky and stood on the earth.

Suddenly the Egyptians were terrified by apparitions in dreams, and anxieties full of foreboding assailed them.

(Wisd. 18:14–17)

These words about the all-powerful word, which comes forth out of deep silence and touches heaven and earth, had always spoken to him in a strange way. They had always penetrated so spontaneously into his soul that he felt himself united with them at a depth that he had not grasped until now. But the immediately following words that spoke of the divine word as a stern warrior who brings destruction and death to the land had remained strange to him, yes even uncanny. Both parts of the passage seemed to belong seamlessly together, yet he did not experience them that way at all. Where did this great difference come from? In any event, since his encounter with the tempter, who brought into full relief the ambiguity of all human signs, he thought the puzzle would soon be solved.

Jesus hearkened to the words of the Scripture while his ear tested them, as the palate tastes food (Job 34:3). Then it happened! A veil was stripped off of the words of Solomon (2 Cor. 3:14). The one all-powerful word separated itself from the many human words. From it an overwhelming light beamed forth. It came from heaven, touched the earth, and penetrated his soul. It illuminated one of Solomon's phrases, while it immersed the others in a contrasting light. The utterance about the stern warrior who brings destruction to the land was now no longer identical with the all-powerful word of God. Previously it had imposed itself on them both, but now an abyss opened up between them. The veil (Isa. 25:7) before his inner eyes that had been torn from the words of Scripture was only an empty mask after the separation. He saw in it the disintegrating image of the tempter. Such delusional phantoms must have risen into the hearts of the Egyptians as they had become troubled and alarmed on Passover night with the exodus of the chosen people (Wisd. 17:13–15).

Yet not only had the pharaoh and the Egyptians been blinded by their own deceptive images, but Israel too had almost always been stiff-necked, and even Moses and Jeremiah had to be reprimanded by

God (Num. 20:12; Jer. 15:19). Even the chosen people created illusions for themselves, for all who heard the word of his Father had never been completely free from darkness, anxiety, and deceptive fantasies. So a perplexing veil had been placed even over the word that came from God. This cover thus made the Scripture scarcely understandable. Jesus revisualized within himself how the all-powerful word descended from heaven in the dark of night, filled everything, and lowered itself into him, until it was one with him. He saw suddenly the image of a thornbush before him out of which a jet of flame blazed up without consuming the bush (Exod. 3:2). He felt like the thornbush. The all-powerful word came from above and rose simultaneously out of his own heart.

Thanks to these new experiences in the wilderness Jesus understood and assimilated what he had heard and what had come over him after his baptism. So now the time had come for him to bear the message of his Father to others. A new sovereignty was pressing forward (Hab. 2:3), and he sensed how he had been caught up since the baptism in an event that would soon lead him further. He lay down once more by the spring. He began softly to sing a psalm, a hymn of thanks for the victory over evil and the new light from above. But suddenly he stopped. What were the words he had just sung?

> **Then the earth reeled and rocked,**
> **the foundations of the mountains trembled;**
> **They quaked, for his anger was kindled.**
> **Smoke rose from his nostrils**
> **and devouring fire from his mouth;**
> **glowing coals flamed forth from him.**
>
> (Ps. 18:7–8)

The glowing coals awoke spontaneously a recollection of the dark redness that wanted to draw him into itself on the mountain. The countenance of the Creator as it was sung in the psalm and the mask of the tempter were quite similar to each other. But it was the countenance of the Lord in his anger. Did this also belong to that dark

veil which was placed over the word of God by sinners? Jesus hesitated and wondered: must not the Holy One be angry with all that is
sinful? This question remained open for him, but it didn't disturb him
because he was filled with a childlike, unspoken trust that his Abba
would lead him further when the moment was right (1 Sam. 16:3).

Meanwhile forty days had passed (Exod. 24:18). On the way back
from the wilderness he considered how he should speak to people and
proclaim the new presence of God with his people. Would his Father work signs as he had often done in the history of Israel? He did
not know what the coming weeks and months would bring. Although
much that was uncertain lay before him, he felt as if he was weightless
and carried along. Some words from a psalm came into his mind:

> **For he will command his angels concerning you**
> **to guard you in all your ways.**
> **On their hands they will bear you up**
> **lest you dash your foot against a stone.**
>
> (Ps. 91:11–12)

The road out of the wilderness led him past a chasm by which he
stopped. For a long time he looked down into the depths where in the
rainy season flowing water fell down between stones and rocks. The
deepness exercised an odd fascination on him. On his pilgrimages to
Jerusalem he had often looked down from the Temple high over the
city (Ps. 68:30) into the Valley of Kidron, and he had seen how the
great band of pilgrims flowed out of the narrow streets of the city into
the open. As he now regarded the depths a shadow suddenly drew
over the sky, and with sharp penetration the words of the psalm that
had accompanied him came to mind. An urgent voice whispered to
him, "Go to Jerusalem and throw yourself down from the pinnacle of
the Temple before the pilgrims, for the angels of God will bear you up
so that your foot does not strike a stone. That will be the sign of your
Father, and the crowd will be amazed and lie in wonder at your feet."

At the sound of the voice as hard as water falling on a stone he
recognized the tempter immediately. He knew that this could not be

the sign about which he asked himself. He wanted to win the hearts of people for his Father and not to evoke the admiring call of the crowd for himself. With great resolve he began to murmur, **You shall not put the Lord your God to the test** (Deut. 6:16). The tempter seemed to dissolve into nothing. As to how he should proclaim his message to people, Jesus left it to the inspiration of the moment. The form of the Son of Man, with whom he knew he had been profoundly one since his baptism and yet whose breath proceeded just ahead of him, guided his steps onward.

God's Sovereignty and Freedom

On his way back to Galilee he saw how the grapes on the vines were opening up and the pomegranate trees were flowering (Song 7:13). He encountered people and talked with them. Filled with the profoundest peace, even joy and exultation, it struck him more than ever how depressed they all were. There were day workers who every morning had to look for work and a wage for their families. Small farmers were nervous about the next harvest. Many sighed under old debts or were marked by illness. The restless glances and the wary probing in conversation betrayed great vulnerability and anxiety in everyone, and the raw, ragged voices witnessed to a life lived in public or private conflict. What powers ruled people? Would they open themselves to the rule of his Father, to his gentle and liberating presence, so finding peace with him and one another? In the time of the prophet Samuel the people had demanded a king in their stiffnecked fashion, although they were told in severely negative images about the oppressive practices of the kings they would have to suffer (1 Sam. 8:1–22). Did humans love servitude to which they could adapt more than the free blowing of the divine breath?

In Galilee Jesus struck out on the way to Capernaum. Already in the first evening after his arrival he went to the square of the small town where as usual people were standing around in groups. Again the depressed faces struck him. Their suffering was impressed upon him and he opened himself deeply within to them. In some groups there was loud laughter, but it was not a liberating laughter. Among others he could see how they put their heads together and whispered. What evil words were beginning their destructive cycle? Suddenly someone began to cry loudly. He hit himself with his fists, threw himself on the ground, and rolled in the dust (Job 10:9). The crowd fell quiet and many pressed around the man who was crying out, while some of them murmured that the evil spirit had seized him again.

Jesus saw how the man lay jerking and tortured on the ground, and at the same time he perceived with all the pores of his body the crowd that stood around, helpless and full of curiosity. Both merged before his eyes into one single picture, and he saw how all of them stood under the force of an alien power and acted like puppets. At that very moment he heard the inner voice, so very clearly, that everything happening around him became a stage on which his Father intended to act. The kindly power that encircled him pushed him to overcome the evil powers. So resolved, he stepped into the middle of the square and called loudly,

Hear, O Israel! The sovereignty of our God is near! The heavy yoke that lies on you is broken and the bar on your shoulders will be taken away (Isa. 9:4). *Our God comes to heal the broken and to free those in chains. To the poor and outcast I bring joyful tidings* (Isa 61:1).

It was still as death in the square, for even the man possessed who lay on the ground was struck dumb. Jesus did not speak long, but soon walked away from the square, left the village, and stepped into the growing darkness of night. The people in the square began to stir as if recovering from a great fright. In the groups that came together again people talked at length about him. Who was he? What did he mean? Was he himself possessed? No one had really understood his words, but many had been strangely fascinated by his voice.

The next evening the people gathered again on the square, and everyone was talking about him. Would he come again? When his

tall form appeared they all suddenly stopped talking. They pressed together and no one dared to get close to him. He looked about for
a long moment. The wretched garments and the rough faces indi-
cated that many day-laborers, small farmers, and beggars were in the
gathered crowd. Their need moved him. He began speaking:

> *Fortunate are you who are now poor, for the kingdom of God be-*
> *longs to you. When your fathers were enslaved in Egypt, the Lord*
> *freed them with his mighty hand. He brought about justice for the*
> *oppressed, and to the hungry he gave bread. He protected aliens*
> *and helped widows and orphans, the poor and downtrodden* (Ps.
> 146:7–9). *Now he has raised his hand anew to come to your aid*
> *and to establish his rule forever* (Ps. 145:13). *Rejoice that you have*
> *nothing and can trust only in him!*

They all stood there stunned, not able to grasp what he said. But
one among them called out, "Will God make us rich so that we can
live with abundance?" Jesus continued:

> *Look at the lilies of the field! Are they not beautiful? And yet they*
> *don't trouble themselves about eating and drinking and clothing.*
> *Learn from them! Have trust like them and then you too will be*
> *cared for.*

A general murmuring began. Many thought he was fantasizing. Of
course it would be nice not to have to work like the flowers of the
field and yet to have everything needed for living. Others conjectured
that he spoke of the reign of the Messiah. Some were quite taken by
his voice and pressed closer to him. One of them was the man who
had cried loudly the day before and writhed on the ground. Even now
he suffered from severe spasms and could walk only with difficulty,
his face contorted. Jesus looked into his rigid, extinguished eyes. He
felt a paralyzing force come upon him, and at the same time he was
moved to help this person who was so miserable. For a moment the
external darkness struggled with the confidence in his heart; then he
saw hope light up in the staring eyes. And it happened: the tormented

man jerked his arms above his head, leaped about, and shouted, "I am healed! He has rescued me!" Then the crowd became excited and everyone crowded around the dancing man. However, Jesus took the opportunity to leave silently.

The next evening everyone waited with great eagerness. Many more people came this time. He arrived at about the same time as the day before and again he saw sad and miserable people before him whose need touched his soul. He spoke to them, responding to their thoughts and feelings:

Don't think the rich and the revelers are fortunate. Your heart is full of lamentation and complaint. Yet you are chosen! God will turn your complaints into dancing. He will take off your robe of lamentation and gird you about with joy. Then your heart will sing and rejoice and thank God. A new joy will adorn Zion, and all that lies in ruins in the land will be built up again. All nations will marvel over your joy and over your God, who appears amidst the glory of his people (Isa. 60:2–11; Jer. 31:4–14).

His words fell like raindrops on the grass and like pearls of dew on the plants (Deut. 32:2); but they still could not soak into the parched earth. Many were touched in their heart but at the same time felt so much more keenly the burden of life that lay on them. There were quite a few this time also who held his words to be those of a dreamer. Some were moved within and wanted to begin dancing.

But most of them stood in hesitation, so that the first steps of those dancing were brought to a halt. Many pushed themselves forward to him. The sick were shoved in front, and he saw their dull expectations, their doubt and questioning hope. Again he felt the paralyzing force in whose sphere the unfortunates lived. As he laid his hand on the first person the tension rose. Again it penetrated the sick like lightning. Many hearts broke out of their hardness and a previously unknown well-being flowed through their bodies. Some began to leap and dance others turned gratefully to Jesus. Those standing around began to speak to one another urgently. What power did he possess?

Had the time really come? Some forced their way through to him and
demanded excitedly, "Is now the time to throw the Romans out of
the land?" He looked at them quietly long enough that their tension
abated somewhat. Then he answered, *Fortunate are they who do not
use violence, for to them God himself will give the land.* The question-
ers stood there noticeably disenchanted and doubtful. How could the
time of salvation come if the pagans were not first driven out?

Only after some days Jesus showed up in Capernaum again. As
soon as he appeared, people came to him full of expectation and curiosity. He sensed their secret anxieties. All their faces were marked
by a life in conflict (Sir. 40:3–5), and everything down to their spon-
taneous gestures betrayed how they were constantly on the watch to
defend themselves against the barbs and arrows of rivals and enemies.
In the evening Jesus spoke to the crowd, who still knew nothing of
peace and joy:

> *The Lord brings peace like a river to Israel* (Isa. 66:12). *He for-
> gives everyone his sins and heals the broken-hearted. He makes the
> deserted vineyards bloom anew and turns the heart of the fathers
> to the sons and the hearts of the sons to the fathers* (Mal. 3:24).
> *Forgive one another, just as the Lord no longer remembers your
> offenses! Blessed are they who work for peace.*

A marked silence followed this speech, for thoughts began to struggle against one another in the hearts of everyone. Perhaps he was
right, but forgiveness must start with the others. While the crowd
waited as if paralyzed, some sick people and women with their children pressed forward to him. Though his speaking had still sparked
no response, he gave himself profoundly over to the desire and distress
of those who came to him. He kneeled down to the little ones, and
a liberating power went from him upon the numerous sick people.
Those healed began to shout and soon they drew the crowd with
them. All the others in the crowd, shaking off their frozen state,
joined in with the enthusiasm. They acclaimed him, but he took ad-

vantage of the press of the throng to withdraw quietly. The day had cost him much of his power.

He walked out into the night. Questions stirred within him, questions which he had to take to his Abba in prayer. Already in the short time of his mission he had been able to perceive how a spark of trust had flashed between the sick and himself. But the same thing had not happened in response to his preaching. The crowd remained trapped in itself, or its mood turned into the kind of enthusiasm that had nothing to do with the peace that the Father wanted to bestow. The power that radiated from him had not sprung over to the hearers and returned to him (Isa. 55:10–11). Why? Must he allow people more time? Would he first have to call individuals in order to make new life experiencable and learnable for the vast throngs by means of a small community?

The Yes of the Disciples and the Rejection in Nazareth

On the next morning he walked along the lake for a long time, crossed over the Jordan, and came into the neighborhood of Bethsaida. He stopped close to fishermen who spent the night outside. He watched them, how they gathered the fish from nets into vessels. For a moment he closed his eyes as the image of ingathering emerged in him with a flow of power. He felt that a decisive moment had come. Meanwhile, the fishermen had taken notice of him and began to talk among themselves about him. Was not this that one who had preached in Capernaum and healed sick people? As Jesus came nearer to them his glance fell on a boat in which two men were at work. They seemed to be brothers. He approached the two of them, looked the one, then the other in the eye (Song 4:9), and said with a warm and full voice, both inviting and challenging: *The reign of God is near. Come, follow me!* The hearts of both men began to beat loudly. Something inundated them, as it were, something they had not known until now. It was anxiety and well-being at the same time. Yet after a moment of shock both responded almost simultaneously and as if in a dream, "Amen."

Jesus turned around. They followed him, and the gaze of the other fishermen went after them.

As he went on, Jesus thanked his Father. For the first time he had sensed that his word had succeeded in truly swaying the hearts of those addressed and had returned to him through their "Amen." But now it was no longer merely his word, for it had awakened an answer in the hearts of both the fishermen, whose names were Simon and Andrew. So now it had became a mutual word. The reign of God, the all-renewing presence of his Father, was in the process of coming.

After a short way with his accompanying travelers who walked silently near him, Jesus came once more upon a group of fishermen. His glance became fixed on a boat in which three men worked, two young ones and one older who must have been the father of the younger ones. Jesus walked decisively up to the group, summoned the word and power of his Father within him, and invited both the young men to follow him. They too joined him after a brief moment of shock and hesitation. The old father, however, was horrified over the sudden departure of both his sons, John and James. But yet in an inexplicable manner he remembered how Scripture recounted that three men had appeared to Abraham at the oak of Mamre (Gen. 18:1–15), and he felt an inner comfort in spite of his shock.

With his four companions Jesus looked for a protected spot where curious looks could not disturb them. He let them lie down on the ground, sat in the middle of them, and said:

> *Humans experience much poverty, grief, and need, but the time of change is near and the rule of God approaches. You have caught and gathered in fish until now. God, however, wants to heal Israel, on whom there is not a healthy spot from head to foot* (Isa. 1:6), *and he intends to gather anew the scattered people in a community of peace* (Isa. 11:12). *So I will make of you fishers of men. Return to your families, do what you need to do for your wives, children, and parents, and free yourselves from family obligations. Before many days I will come back to claim you for myself and the reign of my Father.*

They asked him who he was. But he replied only, *The Son of Man*. They didn't know whom or what he meant by that. But after a moment he added, *The Son of Man is the one who will be with you* (Exod. 3:14), *and you will recognize him*. Then he left them.

Jesus was looking for a garden (Song 6:2) out of which the kingdom of God could grow. Therefore he took the road to his home village. On the way jubilation and thanks filled him that the Father had given him the first disciples. His word had no longer come to nothing in the crowd as had occurred in the initial proclamation. It had awakened life and created a small community which to him was beautiful and full of delight (Song 7:7). As the presence of his Father filled him, he saw himself in a circle of many people, and a word from Scripture came to him:

I am your God and you are my people. (Lev. 26:12)

Nature became alive for him and joined him in his joy. He envisioned pomegranates and henna with nard (Song 4:13), cedars and acacias (Isa. 41:19), cypresses and myrtles (Isa. 55:13). He allowed himself plenty of time in his journey. He healed some sick people on the way and arranged it so that he would arrive in his home village by the Sabbath and could go right away to the synagogue. He was quite moved, and everything in him wondered whether what he would say to the people he knew would receive a full Amen. Would there be a miracle, a miracle of a synagogue community possessed by his Father? He noticed immediately that the eager attention evoked by his presence in the village and in the synagogue was not merely due to his return. News of his new calling had hurried on ahead of him, and they had already heard about his preaching and healings in Capernaum. Curiosity and expectation had seized the village.

After the prayers and the reading from the Torah, the president of the synagogue handed him the scroll of the prophet Isaiah. It turned out to be precisely that passage which had accompanied him on the way:

The Spirit of the Lord God is upon me,
for the Lord has anointed me to bring good tidings to the poor
and to heal all who are brokenhearted,
to proclaim liberty to the captives,
and the freeing of those who are imprisoned,
to announce the years of the Lord's favor. (Isa. 61:1–2)

Here Jesus broke off abruptly because he wanted to pass over the immediate continuation, **a day of vengeance of our God.** He sat down as all eyes were fixed on him. Only then did he feel in full measure how changed he was as he had returned to the village. Before he could always avoid uncomprehending people, but now he must confront them all. They thought they knew him, caught as they were in their dull yet familiar world, but now he must confront them with a message they did not expect from him. Would the word of the Father break in upon the little village-world in which each glanced furtively at the other and where a few of the well-to-do decided what was what? He began to speak. *Today this Scripture of the prophet Isaiah has been fulfilled in your hearing. God sends his Spirit to bring joy to the hearts of the poor and oppressed and to free all those who are bound by the power of evil speech. The time of salvation is breaking in, and I proclaim to you the grace and forgiveness of the Lord.* The men and women in the synagogue gazed with eager looks at the preacher, who seemed to speak according to their expectations. The son of Joseph must have changed into someone great, as many had assumed would happen. Would he now work miraculous signs as he had done in Capernaum? Yet he must especially make his home village famous and the center of his work. In this way everyone would have a part in his success and Nazareth would finally be important in Israel.

Under the expectant looks that were fixed on him Jesus felt that the decisive moment had come. He could easily arouse enthusiasm, which had finally occurred in Capernaum. But if that happened again, the word of his Father would perish. He had to break through the heavy force of their expectations, and so he gathered in himself all the power that flowed into him. Then he went on:

Don't set your hearts on miracles, which are told of the prophets. Be-
lieve the word that comes from God and open your souls to him! As
in the time of Elijah a long drought and a great famine prevailed
in the land, and the prophet did not work a miracle of feeding for
all the poor, but only for a widow, and she was a gentile from
Zarephath in the area of Sidon. Likewise Elisha did not heal all
the lepers who were then in Israel, but only a foreigner, Naaman
the Syrian.

The effect of these words on the people was a sudden stiffening and
an anxious silence. Jesus had run against a mood which was suddenly
changed. Should he speak further? He knew already that his word had
fallen on stony ground and had encountered hearts of bronze and iron
(Jer. 6:28). An intense pain passed through him; but he could not let
down the people who all knew him or betray the task that pressed
him on. So he continued with determination: *I know that no prophet*
is acknowledged in his own country. Now the spell was broken. Unrest
began to spread in the crowd, for in their disappointment the people
put their heads together and began irritatedly to whisper about him.
Did he take them for fools? Apparently he was still unable to perform
any marvelous act and created only words. Jesus heard the whispering
on every side (Ps. 31:13). He closed his eyes, and immediately an
image emerged in his mind: how they would all rise up, lay their curses
on him, and drive him out of the village in order to throw him down
over a cliff. With his whole body he perceived a will to death in the
synagogue (Jer. 26:8–9), which wounded him deeply. Without a word
he got up, looked at everyone without fear and trembling, and walked
slowly past them, while none of them dared to move. He left the
village without even stopping to see his mother, because he couldn't
say anything at this moment which would spare or mitigate her pain.
He must also become even more a stranger to his near relatives (Ps.
69:8). They would succumb to public pressure and stand against him.

When Jesus was outside the village he noticed that someone followed him. It was two afflicted men who tried, with great difficulty,
to catch up with him. One of them had a lame arm and limped, while

the other bore open wounds over his body. With eyes of longing they approached and knelt down before him. He laid his hands on both of them, felt the shaking bodies, and in his heart he lifted up their longing to the Father (Ps. 42:1–2). Again he was able to feel that a power radiated from him. At the same time a stream of fire rose in the sick men out of the depth of their tormented bodies. They jumped up, shouted for joy, thanked Jesus, and rushed back to the village.

Turning back toward Capernaum, Jesus deliberately bypassed the nearby provincial capital Sepphoris, which the sovereign of Galilee, Herod Antipas, had recently established and made his place of residence. Since he knew he was sent to his own people, he didn't want to get involved with the Greek and gentile world. As he traveled, the painful experience in his home village still affected him for a long while. He was now an outcast, and he intuited that behind the forces imprisoning the poor, ill, and troubled people there lurked a dark and destructive will. He felt with soul and body how the reign of God pressed for decision. Would the miracle of word and divine power come to fruition by the sea as had already happened with the sick and those whom he had individually called? Or would the gloomy power of public opinion hold people in bondage, as he had experienced in his home village? Would a whole village, a whole city, even Israel as an entire people let itself be healed? Was his message too great an obstacle for those who knew him from his youth?

The Time of Suspense and Indecision

The great stir caused by his return to Capernaum showed how much they had talked about him during the days that had passed. In the evening the town square was full of people, and they all waited eagerly for him. Before they even noticed his arrival he stood suddenly among them, and right away he began to speak.

Envy not the rich! Happy are you if you hunger and thirst after righteousness. Listen to God and thirst for his word; then you will get rich blessings and become satisfied. Your many cares will be lifted and in peace you will enjoy the fruits of your fields and vineyards (Isa. 65:21). *In your villages and cities joy and hymns of praise will resound* (Jer. 30:19) *and no sword will threaten you. Hunger for the word of the Lord, and each of you forgive the other his debt! The hungry will cease to hunger* (1 Sam. 2:5) *and will celebrate forever.*

The crowd hesitated also this time. A seed of hope had been planted, but at the same time everyone had unanswered questions. Would he actually take away their cares, and what did his message really mean? Why didn't he say more concretely what he intended to do to bring about the marvelous change? Some pressed up close to him untroubled by these questions, above all sick people who had to be led and supported. Jesus felt the hesitation in the crowd and it pained him deeply. However, for the moment he didn't bother with that but opened his soul to the sick who wanted to touch him. He smelled their bodies, heard their gasping breath, and saw signs of anguish in their faces, yet also sparks of hope in their eyes. Their bodies hungered and thirsted for healing and blessing, and this hungering and thirsting resonated completely with his own longing for the coming of the reign of God.

Before he knew it, the sick people began to exclaim about what had happened: "He has healed us! He has healed us!" The cry had a contagious effect, and the hesitation of the crowd turned again into enthusiasm. Many of them pressed close to him, while others — crying and making wild gestures — were talking to each other. Among those who approached him Jesus saw his disciples. He made a way through the crowd to them. He noticed their air of confusion, which meant that in his absence they had begun to doubt. But now the word was alive in them again.

He freed himself from the crowd with them. In the side streets near the square some women followed them and offered them bread and fruits. Jesus took the offerings thankfully for his disciples and himself, and they departed from the town. He spent the night with his disciples for the first time at a place under olive trees which was protected from the wind. While they slept his soul still sought for some time that One whom he loved; and when finally sleep came over him, his heart remained awake (Song 3:1; 5:2).

In the following days they wandered through the villages by the lake and over the mountains and hills of Galilee (Song 2:8). As he had done in Capernaum, he proclaimed the redeeming action of God also in the land of Zebulon and Naphtali (Isa. 9:1).

> He has compassion on the weak and needy,
> and saves the life of the poor.
> From oppression and violence he redeems their life,
> their blood is precious in his sight. (Ps. 72:13–14)

He spoke to the people of the forgiving love of his Father and he appealed to them to become reconciled with each other. The group of those on the road with him grew gradually larger. Some followed him only a few days; others clearly resolved to remain with him. The pressure of crowds was great, and many sick people were granted healing, while some became excited and agitated by his mere presence. From one disturbed man there came forth a cry as soon they came close to him, "Why do you come to disturb us and to destroy us? We know you. You are the Holy One of God." Jesus interrupted sternly, *Be still and leave this poor man!* The madman threw himself on the ground, reared up while crying out, and then lay there completely still. Jesus bowed down, reached out his hand to help him up, and led him immediately back to his family. The healed man wanted to follow, but Jesus turned him back. The people gathered round who had followed all this were thoroughly scared, and as they went on his companions asked him, "Why did the possessed man cry out like that and why did he say 'we'? No one was with him!" Jesus replied, *The hostile power felt itself threatened by the kingdom of God, and it was the power of many in him.* The disciples talked among themselves at length about this response, for they didn't understand what he meant by "many."

On the way Jesus led his disciples, and many other men and women who followed him, up a mountain from which they could look out over large areas of Galilee as far as the lake. After they had eaten the food given to them in the villages, they were all gathered around him. He taught them, and they dared to ask him, "You speak so often of the reign of God. Tell us more exactly—when will it come? How will it be shown and what are we supposed to do?" He looked for a long time at all of them in the circle, paused when his eye fell on certain individuals, and then he began:

You are the light of the world. If you believe with all your soul and all your strength in the word of God, you will be like a city on the hill. It shines and everyone can see it. Remember: as Israel wandered through the wilderness, a cloud pillar moved before them. Every time the cloud rose up over the Tent of Meeting, the fathers set out, and where the cloud stopped, there they set up their camp (Exod. 13:21). As Israel traveled under the cloud, so the reign of God journeys with us and enables us to tread over the heights of Galilee (Hab. 3:19).

The disciples were strangely moved by the way in which he had answered and addressed them. They began to tremble within at the thought that they were a light in the world. Their dreams began to grow like trees in the heights, and one of asked: "When will we see all this with our eyes?" Jesus held the dreams of his disciples back:

Don't be anxious about tomorrow! Forgive whenever one of you has something to rebuke in the other; then you will come to recognize that the reign of God is already in your midst.

The disillusion following these words was evident, and it led, after a long pause, to the question, "You can't repay evil with evil? But the Torah commands an eye for an eye, a tooth for a tooth." Jesus sensed the difficulty for which the Torah was more an excuse than anything else. He began to try to clarify:

Yes, you find that in Scripture; however the kingdom of God cannot come as long as evil always rouses evil and the cycle of retribution continues. God forgives your guilt, but before you pray for forgiveness before him you should also forgive one another.

Once more came a question from the circle: "Will the wicked not triumph if their unjust deeds are not punished?" Jesus noticed that even among the disciples there was resistance to the reign of God, and he sought to convince them with words full of warmth and strength:

Conquer evil through your goodness and you will win the wicked and make them your friends. The old cycle of tit for tat, punch and counterpunch, that leads into the pit of horror will become a new song in your mouth (Ps. 40:2–3).

These words, to which they listened with open ears, enchanted the disciples but nonetheless remained somewhat hard and heavy on their hearts. Cares and hidden anxieties were at work in their souls, not allowing them to be carried into the freedom of the Father. Jesus felt painfully that deep within human beings there were powers at work against the rule of God. Yet all the same, a joyful and unshaken confidence continued to move him to win Israel for the sovereignty and freedom of his Father to liberate it from the powers that enslave.

The Law and the Evil Impulse in the Heart

Since Capernaum lay on the border between Galilee and Gaulanitis, there was a toll station in this town and a garrison of soldiers who watched over public order. The toll officials had to pay rent to the ruler of the region. They had long been in the practice of imposing a duty on those traveling through which was of their own reckoning, beyond the established tariffs. As Jesus was returning to Capernaum and passed by the toll station with his disciples, a man named Levi was sitting there. He was in charge and had a number of assistants working for him. Compelled by a strong intuition, Jesus said to him,

Come, follow me! and went slowly on without waiting for the man's reaction. The head toll official was speechless. Didn't this Jesus belong to those others, the pious ones who despised the tax collectors? Nonetheless, he didn't consider long, but sprang up, gave his place to an assistant, and ran after the group around Jesus. He pushed through to him and said, "I invite you and your disciples to eat with me today." Jesus rejoiced that his word had found a response and accepted the invitation gratefully.

Some Pharisees and scribes, who followed the work of the new preacher with suspicion, observed the whole thing. It was becoming ever clearer to them that he was not on their side. It's true he preached piously and spoke of the God of Israel, but they were growing suspicious because he never clarified all the commands of Moses to the people (Neh. 8:1–8), and he even consorted with those who stood far from the Torah or were unable to understand it at all. On the day after the meal with the chief toll collector they confronted his disciples and asked them reprovingly why they had eaten with sinful tax collectors. Jesus was aware of their approach to investigate him, and he made a public rejoinder: *The physician goes to the ill and not to those who are well, and God calls sinners and not the righteous into his kingdom.* The Pharisees argued, "But the sinners must first be converted" (Zech. 1:3). *Yes, they will be converted,* Jesus answered, *but first of all I want mercy and not sacrifice.*

Others among them followed by saying, "We have also seen that your disciples eat with unwashed hands." He retorted unmoved:

What they ate reached only their stomachs and not their hearts. They were not made unclean by this. Then he continued with a warning: *But what comes out of the human mouth, that is what makes unclean. Out of the heart comes distrustful and evil deeds* (Sir. 37:16). *Be careful about your words!*

After he said this many of the Pharisees and scribes turned in agitation from him and said to each other, "What does this carpenter from Nazareth think he's getting away with? Only those who observe the entire Torah can take the yoke of God's kingdom upon themselves. What he proclaims is suspicious, to say the least. What kind of authority does he have anyway that he hasn't taken any of us as his teacher?" Nonetheless, some among them ventured an objection and pointed to his many healings. Yet others argued to the contrary, that precisely this was suspicious because illnesses were a punishment for sins (Deut. 28:21–22). The sick were required to repent before being healed, but they had never seen this in what he was doing. Were not evil powers at work? They decided to follow his work closely and put it to the test.

The Pharisees and scribes had considerable influence among the ordinary people, and their words aroused suspicion and remained hanging in many ears and hearts (Prov. 18:8). Jesus noticed right away that preaching where they were close by became more difficult. Therefore he withdrew from Capernaum and many followed him, including some scribes and Pharisees. Did they want to spy on him, or had their hearts been touched by the word of the Father? As if led by a cloud pillar, Jesus chose the way into the hills and camped finally in a grove under olive trees. Great tension lay on everyone, for expectation of God's kingdom battled in them with the suspicion that had been spread by the Pharisees.

After a quick meal Jesus turned to the men and women who had followed him:

Don't think I have come to destroy the Torah. God commanded the people through Moses to heed his voice with all their heart and to love him with all their strength. You know the command,

Hear, O Israel! The Lord our God, the Lord is one.
And you shall love the Lord your God with all your heart,
and with all your soul, and with all your strength.
(Deut. 6:4–5)

In just the same way you should conduct yourself with your neighbors. Love them as you would yourselves (Lev. 19:18).

One of the scribes who had followed him interrupted: "That is good and correct, but these two aren't the only commandments. In Scripture there are also many other instructions, and God commanded through Moses to keep the whole Torah." Jesus took up this objection and changed it to an answer expressing God's sovereign rule.

Indeed, you should keep the Torah **wholly.** *Moses strictly forbade you to commit adultery with married women. Yet what goes on in the cities and villages of Israel? When the men stand around together, they gaze at the women with lust, giggle among themselves, and say things which mislead and poison hearts and minds. Haven't you come across what the prophet said?*

> **They have become stallions, well-fed and lusty,**
> **each neighing after his neighbor's wife.** (Jer. 5:8)

Adultery begins in the lustful desire of the heart.

They all looked at him as if struck to the ground. They didn't know what they should think. After a long, painful silence, Jesus continued:

God prohibited you from killing and has consigned murderers to the judgment. Yet what happens in Israel? Every place where they come together — women in the washing place, men in the market — they speak with slippery tongues (Ps. 5:9) about those who are not with them. Suspicions and conjectures are spread around. Don't you see that evil words — like swords between the lips (Ps. 59:7) — penetrate into souls (Ps. 52:1–4)? If your righteousness is not greater than that of the Pharisees and scribes, who are concerned only about the letter of the Torah, then you cannot enter into the kingdom of God.

The hearers were not only struck this time but deeply startled. Most of them involuntarily remembered how they themselves had talked about others who were absent and had condemned them. A feeling of shame began to work in them. Yet at the same time old wounds made themselves felt, wounds they had suffered through wicked words and false suspicions from the mouth of others. In the depths of their injured, convicted souls they sensed the truth of what they had just heard.

Jesus gave them over to their own thoughts while he withdrew to a lonely area. Some of them took the opportunity to return home, for the teaching they had just heard was for them both irresistible and unbearable at the same time. Most of them remained in spite of their perplexity but they could not help but be overcome with contradictory thoughts which battled within them.

After a long interval Jesus turned back to his followers, and the group, now somewhat smaller, gathered about him again. A scribe spoke up: "Master, I've reflected on your words for a long time. You are right; we should love God with our whole heart and put all wickedness against our neighbors out of our hearts. But what about the enemies of God and the adversaries of our people? Moses and the prophets taught that the Lord will repay evil with evil and take vengeance on all his foes. Often his wrath seems even to be without pity. Jeremiah spoke of a coming day of judgment in which those slain by the Lord will lie from one end of the earth to the other (Jer. 25:33), and Isaiah foresaw that that day will be cruel, with wrath and fierce anger (Isa. 13:9). Must we not also condemn and hate those enemies whom God so unrelentingly punishes?"

With this question the scribe voiced a challenge which struck a nerve in all the others. He had expressed what most of them also felt but could not articulate. Jesus allowed the challenge to hang in the circle, until he suddenly said with unexpected decisiveness,

Yes, you have heard that you should hate your enemies. But I say to you: love your enemies and pray for them. Look at the heavenly Father! He makes his sun rise on the good and the evil, and likewise he sends rain on the fields of the righteous and unrighteous. You should act like the heavenly Father.

At first the scribe was dumbfounded by this answer, for he had never heard it in his synagogue. But he quickly recomposed himself and countered with a smugly triumphant voice: "What God has spoken through Moses and the prophets is more important than what sun and rain can teach us." Jesus interrupted him immediately:

Don't you know the word of the Lord?

If I have not established my covenant with day and night and the ordinances of heaven and earth, then I will reject the descendants of my servant David. (Jer. 33:25–26)

Does not the Lord himself tell us that we can recognize his ways from the ordinances of heaven and earth?

The scribe was greatly moved. He marked well that Jesus allowed the Scripture to speak in a way which he did not hear in his synagogue. After a moment of hesitation he left the group in confusion, while some were following him away.

For many who remained with Jesus, that evening turned out to be oppressive and difficult because they could not lay to rest all the questions that had been stirred up. The firm conviction that flowed through the teachings of their master met the resistance of what they had learned from their earliest youth. Even if they did not always follow the Torah and did not even know many of the commandments, yet the words recited to them every Sabbath were still holy. Their hearts hung on them — yes, they even had the feeling that their souls would disintegrate and their bodies would become sick if they gave up the teachings of the Scripture. Of course they had many times remarked that the scribes could also dispute with one another over the meaning of Scripture passages, and it was even told of the pious people at the Dead Sea that they read and revered still other holy books besides Moses and the Prophets. But they all loved those letters and words in the Scripture and based their lives on them. Jesus on the other hand seemed not to be attached to any Scripture and appeared to heed only something in his own inner being. His message was confusing, yet at the same time the power and warmth of his voice released a feeling of freedom in his hearers. But where would this freedom lead them? Would it not be a betrayal of God if they took the voice of Jesus to their hearts and detached themselves from dependence on the holy words of Scripture? Was not anyone who proclaimed another word a false prophet, as Scripture said (Deut. 18:10–20)?

However, not all of those with Jesus were weighed down with such difficult questions. Some of his disciples were rather preoccupied with how things would go if their group became smaller rather than larger.

After nightfall Jesus invited everyone to spend the night in a little hollow under the protection of a cliff (Ps. 18:2). Once more some of them used the opportunity to return home. They were relieved to escape the tension from which they found no exit. The next morning Jesus traveled further over the hills of Galilee with those who had remained with him. They avoided the villages. In spite of that they met people continually. Jesus proclaimed to all these the reign of God and healed those who were sick among them. He let his disciples have time to become more familiar with his message. He repeated many things until they were firmly imprinted on their minds and hearts.

One day certain disciples moaned, "The demands are crushing. We believed at first that the Torah would become lighter through the message of the kingdom of God. But the teachings about adultery in the heart, about hateful speech and love of enemy are terribly hard." Jesus at first only cited a word of the prophet in response to this complaint from the circle of his faithful:

You shall be my people, and I will be your God. (Ezek. 36:28)

Then he asked,

Isn't it wonderful if the name of the Lord resides in the midst of Israel (Ps. 74:7)? But how can his glory dwell in the midst of his people (Ps. 26:8) if at the same time evil thoughts and murderous desires find their home there? How can he grant you blessing and prosperity if you injure and devour each other (Isa. 9:19–20)? The heavenly Father is not terrifying, for he demands only that you open your hearts to him so that he can give you everything. But do you wait for his realm of peace and righteousness?

All of them agreed with him eagerly, while at the same time their hearts remained divided (Ps. 12:2). After some time Simon tried to give expression to his discomfort by asking, "What should we do if others continually offend us. Should we forgive them seven times?" Simon intended to name an improbably high number. He was stunned, however, to hear Jesus respond:

Why seven times? Think back to the beginning of the world! When Cain murdered Abel a sevenfold revenge was threatened for every murder thereafter (Gen. 4:15). But even that did not hold, for soon already Lamech would say to his wives Adah and Zillah:

> **If Cain is avenged sevenfold, then truly Lamech seventy-sevenfold.** (Gen. 4:24)

And only a generation later, in the time of Noah, the whole earth became corrupt and full of violence (Gen. 6:11). Evil had increased from the first sin on, and it filled the whole earth like a great flood (Gen. 7:17–24). How can such a power be overcome if the love of God and neighbor is not at least as strong? Simon, if Lamech was avenged seventy-sevenfold, then you should forgive seventy-sevenfold.

Simon stood there speechless. What he heard was partly like a dream and partly like a dark burden.

One day John asked, "If evil is so mighty in the world, shouldn't we set out in a great war against it?" In reply Jesus asked only, *Where will you battle it?* John fell into embarrassed silence. Thomas spoke up: "Jeremiah speaks of the evil impulse in the heart (Jer. 7:24–28)." *Indeed, Jeremiah is right,* sighed Jesus.

The human heart is stubborn and rebellious (Jer. 5:23).

Can an Ethiopian change his skin
or a leopard his spots?
Then also you can do good
who are used to doing evil.

(Jer. 13:23)

How will Israel repent of its own strength, since no leopard can change its spots? Earlier it ran after false gods (Jer. 7:9) and imitated the abominations of foreign nations (Deut. 18:9), and today each one eyes his neighbor and does whatever seems to bring himself glory. But this is not what the honor and glory of God seeks.

The disciples were depressed as they listened to this. Suddenly, however, the voice of their master was changed, and they heard words which reached their hearts:

God is greater than the human heart. You know the promise:

A new heart I will give you and a new spirit I will put within you. And I will take out of your flesh the heart of stone and give you a heart of flesh. (Ezek. 36:26)

The time for the fulfillment of this promise is here. Haven't you often experienced in Capernaum and on the road how people possessed by evil powers became liberated through the approach of God's kingdom? Let your own hearts also be healed!

With these words most of them felt as though something hot was tearing through their chest, for within them a clamp began to loosen which they had scarcely noticed before because it was so completely a part of their life. Jesus sensed the bursting open of their hearts and the welling up of feelings in his disciples and the women who accompanied him. If he let them alone the new experience would move through them fully. So he began softly to sing a psalm of praise and thanksgiving in which everyone slowly joined. The simple and sustaining melody gathered in what broke up and flooded through them.

Together they repeated other such hymns, which rose up over the hills to the heights of heaven and in which the great tension of the recent days could be released. They immersed themselves in praise and thanks, by which they let their souls ride on the wings of the wind (Ps. 18:10). Mountains and hills, trees and shrubs, even the dry and stony paths seemed to share their gladness (Ps. 89:12). The voice of the turtledove was heard in the land (Song 2:12). As the long and eventful day drifted away and the shadows of evening grew (Song 4:6) they camped in a vineyard with henna shrubs and the fragrance of myrrh plants (Song 3:6). The cool air lay on them like a great sheltering peace, and the beginning of night covered them, so that anxiety did not disturb their dreams.

Spontaneous Love and Demonic Suspicion

In Capernaum anxiety and eagerness were in the air as they returned to the town on the lake. Scribes and Pharisees must have zealously spread rumors and further suspicions about him. Yet not everyone thought the same, for one of the Pharisees invited him and his disciples to his house. When the hour of the meal arrived, they reclined, as was the custom, on cushions placed around the lower tables. During the meal the host devoted himself to seeing that everything was in order. It was important to him that he make a good impression. Suddenly, however, Jesus noticed that someone approached from behind. Tears fell on his feet which soon became more abundant. He sat up and saw a woman looking at him whose eyes were full of anxiety and loving openness. He felt her distress and longing, and as she bent down he let her dry his feet with her long hair. Feeling the kisses of her warm mouth, he felt certain of the love and honor she wished to show him. Here was a heart completely open to what he wanted to bring and proclaim. This woman expected no healing like many sick people, neither had he called her as he had his disciples. Now she even anointed his feet with fragrant nard (Song 1:12).

The host, who lay directly across from Jesus, followed closely the entire incident. He could see the woman well in back of his guest, and Jesus read what he was thinking from his eyes. The woman had to be especially suspect from his standpoint. Jesus, however, didn't let this suspicion bother him. To the contrary, the more he was struck by the Pharisee's distrust, the stronger he felt the woman's reverence and trust and her harmony with the rule of God. He posed a question to the surprise of the host: *Which debtor will love his master more, the one who is forgiven a small sum or the one who is forgiven a large debt?* The Pharisee was unprepared for this. He answered, without taking long to consider, "Certainly that one who is forgiven the large sum." Jesus straightened up and said before all the dinner guests of the Pharisee, *You have seen the signs of love this woman has shown me; but you have shown me none of them. Her love must be greater. Doesn't it follow from your own words that she is likewise forgiven much?* Without waiting for an answer, he turned to the woman with a tenderness in his voice which corresponded to what he had felt from her: *So it is, your sins are forgiven you.*

The meal came abruptly to an end. Everyone stood up and began to talk heatedly to one another in small groups. Some of his disciples knew the woman and were astonished at the conduct of their master. The relatives of the Pharisee gathered about him, and one person shouted indignantly, "What he's doing is unheard of. You invited him, and yet he showed preference to this whore over you before all your guests." A scribe spoke up who also belonged to the kinfolk of the Pharisee: "Not only that, it's outrageous that he dared to forgive sins. Who can forgive sins except God alone?"

Jesus knew that after this evening the talk about him in Capernaum would be even more furious and agitated. So he withdrew once more from the border town and wandered along the bank of the lake into the neighboring villages. He was preoccupied with an all-important question. On the one hand, the suspicion and rejection of the Pharisees and scribes was growing, while on the other the woman at the dinner party made him feel that in spite of human sin there were persons who were ready to accept him and his message with wakened hearts. Would the sparks of the kingdom of God still spring up? Would the fire begin to burn that he wanted to set in Galilee? Frequently he let his disciples go by themselves while he spent many hours in prayer with his Father. His soul hurried through secret gardens; he perceived the one who came for the breeze of the day (Gen. 3:8) and heard the voice that addressed him as the beloved son. Wells of living waters flowed in him (Song 4:15).

In Magdala, a fortified city on the west bank of the lake where great quantities of newly caught fish were salted and prepared for sale in Jerusalem and even in Rome, a young woman in untidy clothes and disheveled hair came toward him. She came from a well-to-do family and had seven brothers who had disdained her since she was a child. She screamed and cursed at Jesus, then collapsed suddenly upon him, fell down before him, and grasped his feet while foam was appearing on her lips. He bent down and with a strong hand he pulled her to her feet. He saw before him a rigid and contorted face. Yet behind her restless eyes shone something like two doves (Song 4:1). A dark power cried from within her, "Don't trouble us!" He asked the possessed woman, *Who are you?* The answer in a strained voice was, "We are seven." The young woman tried to tear away, but Jesus held her fast before releasing her. He looked up to his Father, felt the resistance in her that sought to paralyze her, and gave himself completely over to the liberating power that comes from above. Suddenly words came to his lips as if by themselves: *Release her!* Trembling ran through her body, she sank to the ground and began to weep loudly. Her whole body shook with sobs. Jesus crouched down beside her and held her hand until she quieted down and could stand again. After he learned that her name was Mary, he sent her back to her family.

News of the healing of the possessed daughter of the prominent family ran like wildfire through Magdala. A large number of people assembled in the evening on the city square and Jesus spoke to them.

The God of our fathers led our ancestors out of bondage in Egypt. He comes also today with mighty arm to free you from slavery to the evil powers. Trust with your whole heart in the heavenly Father and let his kingdom come to you!

The expectation was great among some in the crowd. Some thought he must be the long yearned for Messiah, otherwise he couldn't have healed the wild and possessed Mary. However, many others came only out of curiosity, and since their businesses were going well they felt no need to be freed from bondage.

But a larger group, which included many scribes, separated openly from him. They had furious discussions and were saying that the Egyptian diviners and priest-magicians had also worked miracles with the help of the devil (Exod. 7:11, 22). Jesus walked up to the hostile group. But before he could speak to them, someone threw up to him this accusation: "You can drive out the evil spirits only in alliance with the prince of demons." He was startled, for he had never heard such an objection. These words with harmful intent pierced him like arrows, but in spite of them he found quiet words for his opponents: *Do you truly believe that demons cast out demons? How can the kingdom of Satan endure if it destroys itself?* Since they were silent, he continued: *If you suspect and reject my works, isn't there nonetheless something good in them which you should not make into a devil? Consider carefully! If I drive out the evil powers by the might of God, then his kingdom is here and now arriving.* They remained silent in their stiff-necked fashion, so he made another attempt: *You understand how to interpret the clouds in the sky and you know when rain comes and when it will be hot. Why can you not understand the signs of the times?* Since a hostile silence was still their only response, he withdrew from them. Because of the three rejections (Amos 1:3) and their hardness of heart, he was deeply affected.

The Twelve in Action for Israel the Accused

Jesus didn't want to go to the newly constructed Tiberias, which Herod Antipas established as the capital of Galilee. Therefore he left the lake route, as the Son of Man led him. The sovereign of Galilee, in contrast to his father, was respected by the nobles because he had brought about a degree of peace and order in Galilee through clever tactics, and thus he had seen to it that numerous landowners, merchants, and small business people were able to become well-to-do. Jesus was well aware of the sly fox and preferred to avoid him for the time being, although the wife of one of Herod's officials had reported to him that the ruler would like to see him perform a miracle. He chose the route into the middle of Galilee. Mary of Magdala, who could hardly be recognized from her former appearance, followed him and his disciples.

The Pharisees of the wealthy city had ascribed to him signs of the devil. He knew their zeal and that they meant only to remain faithful to the holy Torah. How was it that evil was ascribed to him? Why was the victory over the dark powers that his Father had given him condemned by them as the work of the prince of demons? How could this dark realm, in which many hostile powers were at play, be turned upside down? This question pushed him to double his efforts for the rule of his Father. His disciples often fell into doubt, yet a new peace had begun to work in them. Should he draw them into his mission of proclamation? Would the trust involved in sharing his task with them open their hearts without reservation, which were still partially divided? Would they then help set the land afire, something he so fervently awaited?

He took the way to Mt. Tabor (Judg. 4–5). As he stayed awake overnight by himself on the mountain, he gave over his concern for the kingdom completely to his Father. On the next morning he called his disciples to him and selected from them twelve corresponding to the ancient tribes of Israel (1 Kings 18:31). He commissioned them to go before him into the villages and to proclaim the kingdom of God as they had heard it from him. They were stunned by this commission they received so unexpectedly from their master. Anxiety seized them. Yet at the same time his trust in them gave them a confidence which urged them on, so that they soon ventured out on the way. As they descended from the height into the valley, Jesus gazed after them for a long time. They were going there like the twelve tribes of Israel. Hope rose in him, and the words of the seer Balaam came to him, the one who had spoken with eyes closed, yet simultaneously uncovered:

> How fair are your tents, O Jacob,
> your encampments, O Israel!
> Like valleys stretching afar,
> like gardens beside a river,
> like oaks the Lord has planted,
> like cedars beside the waters.
>   (Num. 24:5–6)

Would the miracle occur and the people change from an overgrown vineyard (Isa. 5:4–7) to the residence and garden of God? In prayer he accompanied the preaching of the twelve from Mt. Moreh, which lay across from Mt. Tabor. He identified himself so completely with their journey that in a mysterious way he shared their fate. All at once he remembered how a mask was stripped off the holy writings during his days in the wilderness. Soon the bad and suspicious words of the scribes and Pharisees of Magdala vanished in his soul.

While the twelve preached in the villages a mysterious struggle accompanied them. An evil power disguised as one of the sons of God sought to sow deception. It wanted to keep people far from God and it complained constantly before him (Job 1:6–2:7). Jesus knew that his Father would not listen to the spirit that sowed distrust. Something suddenly occurred to him, taking him by surprise. He saw that the sky over Galilee was immersed in a dusky light (Wisd. 17:19–20) and light remained only in the place where he was. Then the darkness was loosened like a mask from the sky, rolled into a ball, and became a dark red tail of fire. Satan, the great accuser, fell like a lightning-flash onto the earth, and the whole sky was bright once more. The countenance of his Father illumined once more the way that his disciples followed through the villages of Galilee. The freeing of heaven moved Jesus deeply, and he gave thanks. Had the rule of his Father, which pressed him on since his baptism in the Jordan, now fully broken in? Would it awake and attract the tired hearts of human beings, or would the overthrow of the great accuser from the heavenly world only intensify the condemnation and destruction on earth (Rev. 12:10)?

A great yearning welled up in him to learn quickly how the disciples were doing since the collapse of Satan. He hurried after them. In the villages of Zebulon (Isa. 9:1) he passed through he noticed quickly that there was preparation for his coming. However, the decisive change for which he was waiting had not come to pass. When he was once more with the twelve they recounted joyfully to him what they had done and that even demons had been made to obey them. Jesus listened closely and deeply to what they told him in order to get a sense of how his Father had accompanied their preaching. Might they be able to hear that inner, sweet voice (Song 2:14) which led him and caused everything in the world to open and blossom? But they seemed to rejoice primarily in having been able to exorcise demons from some persons who were possessed. As he questioned them they acknowledged that they had often experienced rejection and were ridiculed. Jesus opened their eyes to the battle that had secretly accompanied their work:

I saw Satan fall like lightning from heaven. So now demons must obey you. But now the fallen accuser tries all the harder to confuse men on earth and to goad them on against one another. The battle has only begun. But rejoice anyway, for you are chosen for the kingdom and the heavenly Father has called each of you by name.

Withdrawal and Signs of Faith among Gentiles

When Jesus returned to Capernaum he didn't speak again in the public square, although he went as usual to the synagogue on the Sabbath. He sat down unobtrusively, but the attention of all was directed toward him. Then the prayers portions from the Torah and other Scriptures were read, and everyone heard how Moses, by God's commission, commanded them to sanctify the Sabbath. In the sermon that followed, the leader of the synagogue, a Pharisee, explained what had been read. In the course of his comments he turned suddenly with a challenge directed to Jesus: "Is it allowed to heal on the

Sabbath?" Close to the president there sat a man who had long had a paralyzed arm. Jesus answered with a counterquestion: *Is it allowed to do good on the Sabbath?* The president responded, "Six days of the week are for work. On them one helps and heals others. The Sabbath, however, is holy. On it we are commanded to rest, as the Lord ordained, for he himself explained that the seventh day was holy after six days of creation, and he rested on it" (Gen. 2:2–3). The preacher's answer impressed everyone in the synagogue; Jesus, however, continued undeterred: *Don't you untie your oxen and donkeys from the stable on the Sabbath and lead them to wells so they can quench their thirst? If the animals should not suffer on the Sabbath, why then should human beings?* Then he repeated his first question, *Is it allowed to do good on the Sabbath?* The president had nothing to say, and likewise the other Pharisees and scribes who were present had nothing to answer. Jesus looked at them full of concern and sadness. For a moment he closed his eyes to let the whole commotion and tension around him melt away. As he listened to his inner voice, the image of the man with the paralyzed arm rose up before his eyes and he perceived the will of the Father. He commanded the handicapped man to stand in the middle of the gathering, and he came forward trembling. Jesus glanced once more at the tense, silent congregation; then he spoke with a voice full of authority: *The Son of Man is Lord of the Sabbath.* When he touched the man he jumped as if startled and threw both arms in the air. A great tumult started, and the worship service broke up in an uproar. Many of the simple people were astonished and praised God for the miracle.

However, a group of Pharisees and scribes gathered in order to take counsel. Since the arm of the man had long been lame, there was no necessity at all of healing him precisely on the Sabbath. The so-called prophet from Nazareth could have — if he really held the Torah to be holy — healed him easily earlier or later. So their judgment was finally clear: he must be a false prophet allied with evil powers. The adherents of Prince (Tetrarch) Herod, particularly wealthy landowners and merchants, affiliated themselves readily with the opinion of the Pharisees. For them Jesus was one of those unpredictable preachers — like the

Baptizer at the Jordan River — who popped up again and again and threatened to disturb public order. Their experience led them to rely on the Pharisees and scribes, for this party held the religious fanatics under control.

Jesus avoided direct confrontation and turned back with his company to the neighboring village Chorazin. From there he wandered through the villages of Naphtali and the area on the other side of the Jordan (Isa. 9:1). He began to proclaim the kingdom of God above all in parables:

> *A sower went out to his small field which lay on the slope of a hill. When he sowed seed, some fell on the path, others among the stones or thorns; only a remnant (Isa. 10:20–22) fell on good soil. The seeds on the path were immediately devoured by birds. The seeds among the stones or thorns did grow at first, but then they were wilted by the hot sun or choked by the thorns. Only the seeds falling into the good ground bore abundant fruit — yes, fruit in superabundance.*

Many hearers, who had expected a miracle rather than a parable, or who were simply curious as to how his dispute with the Pharisees and scribes would continue, asked disappointedly, "What does he mean with this story? We don't need to be told that seed sown on a path or among stones or thorns cannot produce any fruit." But Jesus didn't explain the parable to them.

As they traveled his disciples confessed that they too had not understood his parable. In response he led them step by step to an initial insight. *Haven't you noticed what has happened in the past weeks and months and what you yourselves have experienced?* They looked at one another, astonished and puzzled.

> *Remember the days when you proclaimed God's reign in the villages! For many hearers the word was received only superficially, and the evil spirit immediately stole it from them again. Others received it at first with joy, but then came doubts or worries and the word was stifled. Some joined us and soon left us. Among some,*

however, it fell into their heart and struck deep roots. Indeed, the kingdom of God is like a mustard seed. When it is sown in the ground it is the smallest of all seeds. Yet as soon as it grows to maturity it towers over all other growing things and becomes even a tree in which the birds of the sky can nest. Have you ever seen mustard seeds?

They answered, "No, only mustard plants." He answered, *It's like this that the power of God works miracles; much is possible for faith, but you don't comprehend this yet.*

The idea of the power of God that can work miracles gave renewed impetus to the fantasies of the disciples. As they traveled they discussed heatedly how the kingdom of God would break in with power. Would the Romans and all pagans be expelled by angels and the wicked scribes be punished? Would abundance prevail, and would their master be the awaited king of peace (Isa. 9:6–7)? Above all, however, they wondered what place they themselves would assume in the new kingdom. Jesus noticed the height of expectancy to which they had risen, and he told them a further parable.

A rich landowner sowed wheat seeds in his field. In the night his enemy came and sowed weeds among the good seeds. As the latter grew, the bad growth also appeared. The servants of the landowner asked their lord whether they should pull out the weeds. He replied to them, "No, for you might damage the wheat. Only at the harvest shall you tear out the weeds and burn them."

He left it to the disciples to find the sense of this parable. But in spite of a long discussion they couldn't agree on an interpretation. The next day he explained to them: *The evil spirit sows false thoughts even in those who receive the word of the kingdom of God in their hearts. God allows both to grow so as not to destroy the good plants in rooting out the weeds. Watch out, in case the evil enemy sows weeds also in you!* The disciples were struck by this interpretation. One of them, however, was dissatisfied; he took into himself everything he heard to test it in the future.

Although Jesus still spoke to the people only in parables and the dwellers in the villages listened to him in perplexity, many sick people came to him just as they had earlier. He gave himself unrestrictedly to their distress and lifted up their longing for healing before his Father. With each healing he felt that some part of the weight of the liberated person was laid on him and that the burden was becoming ever heavier. He remembered that Moses also had to bear the rebellious people in the wilderness and complained that it was too heavy for him alone (Num. 11:14). Also the prophetic words of the Servant of God, on whom the Spirit of the Lord rested and who bore the illnesses and the suffering of the people (Isa. 53:4), became clearer to him. He too had experienced the Spirit of the Lord on him since his baptism. Was it now also his task to bear the sicknesses and suffering of the people by himself (Matt. 8:17)?

As he proceeded slowly with his disciples toward the north, he came into the land of Dan (Judg. 18:11–31). The more gentiles there were in the villages, the less he preached and the more he turned his attention to the disciples. It was urgent for him to find out how much they sensed and understood about the voice that led him. When they entered the district of Caesarea Philippi, where Philip, the brother of Herod Antipas, had had his residence built, he ventured a deeper encounter with them. Once again he began indirectly and asked them what others, the people in Galilee, said about the Son of Man. "Various and great things people speak of you," they answered. "Because you work miracles, some take you for John the Baptist, whom Herod executed but whom God raised from the dead. Others see you as Elijah, who is to return at the end of days (Mal. 4:5–6). Others think you're a prophet, like Isaiah, Jeremiah, or Ezekiel." That the Pharisees judged him to be a false prophet they passed over, for they didn't dare repeat their angry, derogatory statements. With these responses Jesus confirmed once more the extent to which even those of good will among his hearers judged by what was familiar to them, and how little they had surmised about him and the mystery of the voice that led him.

But where did the disciples stand, those who had followed him in spite of many persecutions? He posed the question directly to them: *But who do you say I am?* They looked anxiously at one another, until Simon spoke up for everyone: "You are the Messiah, whom God with his might has anointed." Jesus let the answer hang as if in the air for a long time. He was grateful for the recognition that had lighted in them, and at the same time he felt a shadow lying on him. He lifted his eyes on high and prayed aloud, *I praise you, Father, that you have concealed this from the wise and clever scribes, but have revealed it to simple fishermen. Yea, Father, it has pleased you to let your word come to mankind in an inconspicuous fashion.* Immediately then he turned to his disciples and forbade them strictly to speak publicly about the Messiah. Along with the joy sadness also filled him, for he remembered his experience in his home village, where they thought they knew him but for precisely that reason had rejected him from the very beginning. Would the disciples also remain at the level of knowledge which had been given them? Would familiarity hinder them from hearing what they did not yet know? He prayed for them to the Father.

He let himself be led by the Son of Man, with whom he was completely one, but yet who went before him. The cedar trees reached from the mountains of Lebanon (Ps. 104:16) down to the way they traveled. Prophetic images of the messianic time emerged and accompanied them:

> The wilderness and the dry land shall rejoice,
> the steppe shall shout for joy and blossom. . . .
> The glory of Lebanon shall be given to it,
> the majesty of Carmel and the Plain of Sharon.
>
> (Isa. 35:1–2)

On the wooded way things became quite peaceful, and the people in the area didn't usually seem to know the wandering group. They were alone by themselves, so the tensions of the recent weeks left all of them. The joy of the messianic time, which had never departed from deep in Jesus' heart, became foremost once more as he gazed on the mountains and cedars. He recited a psalm with his disciples:

> You brought a vinestock out of Egypt,
> You drove out the nations and planted it.
> You cleared the ground for it;
> it took deep root
> and filled the land.
> Its shade covers the mountains,
> its branches the cedars of God.
> It sent out its branches to the sea....
>   (Ps. 80:8–11)

They followed the shoots of the vineyard in the direction of the sea, which soon caused new images to spring up in them. Heaven and earth glorified the Lord, and also the sea with everything that moved in it (Ps. 69:34). In the raging and roaring of the waves they heard the raving and raging of the peoples (Isa. 17:12), and in the revolt of Rahab the sea monster (Ps. 89:9–10) they saw mirrored the chosen people who would not hear the good news. But God showed himself to them as the Lord over all.

> The floods have lifted up, O Lord,
> the floods have lifted up their voices,
> the floods lift up their roaring.
> Mightier than the roaring of many waters
> mightier than the breakers of the sea,
> the Lord on high is mighty! (Ps. 93:3–4)

They came into the district of Zarephath (1 Kings 17:8), which lay between Tyre and Sidon. There suddenly a woman came running after them. She must have heard of Jesus and his deeds, although she was not a Jew. She exclaimed: "O Lord, son of David, have mercy on me. My daughter is tormented by demons." He paid no attention to the woman. However, she followed him tenaciously and didn't let up her loud crying and pleading. Since she didn't cease her loud crying, the disciples urged their master to give in to her. But he refused decisively: *I have been sent to gather only the lost sheep of Israel.* The woman meanwhile pushed her way completely to him, fell at his feet, and begged him yet more urgently: "Lord, help me." Jesus had in view the election of Israel and his mission, but the woman would not understand that at all and in her distress would also not be able to understand a long explanation. So he felt he must, even at the cost of being offensive, make his task clear with drastic words: *It isn't right to take away bread from the children and throw it to the dogs.* The severe words pained him, and he steeled himself for a bitter reaction.

But what a surprise! The woman acknowledged that he was right, but reacted instinctively in a way that he himself had done toward his opponents. She took his own words and turned them against him: "But even the dogs get some of the scraps that fall from the table of their masters!" Jesus was amazed, recognizing suddenly something of the voice that led him in the words of this woman. Didn't a faith live in her which he had so painfully missed until now in his own people? He opened himself to her: *Woman, your faith is great. What you desire shall happen.*

After this event Jesus asked himself whether the Father was calling him to the gentiles. He considered the prophetic promises, that many peoples with all their riches would travel up to Jerusalem to worship the true God (Isa. 60:1–62:12). Did his Father want first to transform the lips of a pagan people into clean lips in order to make Israel jealous (Zeph. 3:9)? In prayer he gave over all uncertainty to his Father and waited for the answering voice. Yet it soon became clear to him that he must remain with his people, although it was stubborn and had plugged ears and eyes glued together (Isa. 6:10).

They chose the way of the sea (Isa. 9:1) for the journey south, and at times they walked in the soft sand along the shore. Jesus asked his disciples how many grains of sand lay on the shore. They looked at him oddly. Was his question meant seriously, or what was he trying to do? He let them in on something of great meaning to him.

Remember Abraham and the promise which he received after the confirmation of his obedience!

I will indeed bless you and make your descendants numerous as the stars in heaven and the sand on the seashore. (Gen. 22:17)

But where are the innumerable descendants of Abraham today? Israel is a small nation and the kingdom of God begins like a grain of seed. Yet think about the gentile woman of Zarephath! Have faith like her and the reign of the Father will reach out to people without number!

The disciples took from this renewed hope that a kingdom would come to be out of their circle.

Soon after their arrival in Capernaum some Jewish elders sought out Jesus. They were sent by a Roman centurion who commanded a division of soldiers there. They came with the request that Jesus heal his sick servant. For their part, the elders begged Jesus to fulfill the wish of the centurion; for though he was a pagan, he loved the Jewish nation and had even had a synagogue built. Jesus recalled the woman of Zarephath and went with the elders. But even before he came to the house, further messengers appeared, who said for the centurion, "Lord, do not trouble yourself, for I am not worthy to receive you in my house. I obey those in authority over me, and I have soldiers under me who likewise execute every order I give them. So speak only a word and my servant will be healed." Jesus was astonished, for this Roman centurion, despite his high position, disclosed a humility and a trust in him similar to that he had found in the gentile woman. He turned to the Jewish elders who accompanied him and said, *Not even in Israel have I found such faith. Follow the example of this gentile soldier, and Israel will find salvation!* They were embarrassed and had nothing to say, and they turned away from him. But the centurion's servant was restored to health.

This last appeal had fallen on deaf ears. Jesus climbed with his disciples up a hill from which they could look over Capernaum and the

villages north of the lake. There he prayed and he sang in company
with them:

> Let the hills bear peace for the people
> and righteousness the hills. . . .
> May [the king] be like the rain on the fields,
> like showers that water the earth!
> May righteousness bloom in his days,
> and great peace abound, till the moon be no more!
>
> (Ps. 72:3, 6–7)

He looked over the mountains and hills of Galilee and asked, *Why
have peace and righteousness not come down upon them?* Individuals
had begun to hear. Nevertheless, all the villages and towns resisted his
call. The proclamation of the arriving reign of God provoked a new
hardening of hearts.

Second Act

Judgment and Self-Imprisonment in Evil

As Jesus left Galilee and crossed over the lake, a threatening clattering and thundering, like a troop of calvary swiftly approaching (Hab. 1:8), could be heard, and entire kingdoms seemed to rush out in the whistling of the sharp wind (Isa. 13:4). The water piled up in high waves and fell back into the deep. He had sown the word in the mountains and valleys of his home region; but the ears of the villagers were plugged so as not to hear and the eyes of the town-dwellers were closed so as not to see (Isa. 6:10).

In his company were the twelve, other men and women disciples, and some scribes and Pharisees who, deeply impressed by the work of the preacher from Nazareth, did not want to follow the judgment of rejection made by their brothers in faith. While they looked back to the villages and towns from a high place on the other side of the lake he gave free course to his pain:

Woe will come to you, Chorazin and Bethsaida. In the region of Tyre and Sidon I have found faith without the working of miracles. You, however, have seen many miracles and still have not believed. And you, Capernaum? In you the kingdom of God would strike roots and from its vines it would begin to work out of you. You would have grown up as high as heaven, but now you are like the godless ruler who wanted to ascend to heaven and establish his throne in the north over the stars (Isa. 14:13). Like him, you will be flung into the depths of the abyss. A judgment will strike you which will be more destructive than the fire on Sodom and Gomorrah.

He had always experienced his God as a tender presence, and now with a glance at his ministry these severe words had come to his lips as if by themselves. The opposition had changed his message. The disciples were agitated by this new message. While some experienced anxiety, John and James, the sons of thunder, evinced their deep passion: "Perhaps a fire will soon fall from heaven and destroy all our opponents."

Blood on the Hem of Their Garments

They were walking now in the direction of Jerusalem, and a promise of great success was still felt by some disciples. They were saying, "In Jerusalem things will go better." These words touched a deep pain in Jesus. While proclaiming the kingdom in Galilee he had always thought in terms of Israel as a whole. He didn't want — like Jeroboam in Bethel and Dan (1 Kings 12:26–33) — to split the people over their sanctuaries, but to gather them in Zion and Jerusalem. He had already encountered the spirit of this city, for which the heart of all Galilean pilgrims throbbed, in Nazareth and Magdala, in Chorazin and Bethsaida, and above all in Capernaum. So the lament broke from deep within him:

> *Jerusalem, city chosen and called for peace,*
> *you kill the prophets and stone the messengers who are sent to you.*
> *I would lead your sons home from afar*
> *and gather your daughters from the end of the earth* (Isa. 43:6);
> *yet you would not.*
> *Therefore will your streets and houses*
> *be empty and become desolate.* (Jer. 7:14–15)

He spoke with such a strange voice that all who heard him were more surprised and shocked than by what he said about the Galilean villages and towns. What had been said in these words? Why did he condemn the holy city to which they were only now underway?

One of the scribes couldn't contain himself. "Master, your judgment is incomprehensible and severe. In Jerusalem no prophet will be slain." At this objection great tension swept over the group, until Jesus turned to the scribe and said,

> *Have you not heard that King Manasseh filled the city with blood* (2 Kings 21:16) *and had the prophet Isaiah sawed in half? Zechariah son of Barachiah was even murdered between the sanctuary and the altar* (2 Chron. 24:17–21). *And it was scarcely better for Jeremiah, for the priests and prophets of the city sought to execute him* (Jer. 26). Then he turned to all of them and continued: *God has continually sent prophets to warn Israel and lead it back to him.*

> **Yet they killed the prophets and committed great blasphemies.** (Neh. 9:6)

> *Therefore the Lord must speak to Jerusalem, the holy city, as judge — as judge to her whom he himself chose when she was a small, blood-smeared little girl and whom he married in the time of love* (Ezek. 16:1–6):

> **A city that sheds blood in the midst of her, that the time of judgment may come, and makes idols to defile herself! You have become guilty through the blood you have shed and defiled by the idols you have made.** (Ezek. 22:3–4)

For the company around Jesus it was as if the prophet Ezekiel himself had spoken. After a moment when his words had faded away, Jesus asked the scribe who had raised an objection against him, *Why do you hold my judgment to be wrong if you believe the prophet? Have I said anything different from Ezekiel?* The scribe, who felt his honor challenged, was an intelligent man and knew all the passages Jesus had cited. They had already struck him earlier on, and he had worked out a position through zealous study of Scripture. "All the passages you have taken up refer to the time when God used the king of Babylon as a hammer (Jer. 51:20–23) in order to judge his own people and to destroy Jerusalem. However, in distant exile Israel turned to its God wholeheartedly (Bar. 1:15–2:35), as King Solomon had already prophesied (2 Chron. 6:36–39). Since then the nation has improved. The prophets announced judgment against Jerusalem because there was much idolatry in the city during the time of the kings. Today, however, there is neither tribe nor clan, neither district nor town which worships gods made by human hand (Jud. 8:18). Only the gentiles serve demons, and so they are the ones, not Jerusalem, who will be subject to severe judgment."

Jesus interrupted the scribe, who was caught up in zeal and defended himself with all his knowledge.

> *Do only the gentiles serve demons? Why then are there so many sick and possessed people in Israel? There are other idols than those made of wood or stone; for many of them are established in the heart and honored there. These are the worst ones. When I expelled demons some were saying that the Son of Man has an alliance with the prince of demons. Whom did they serve who made such a judgment?*

Although the scribe had not completely understood the last part of what Jesus said, he had become somewhat more insecure. All the same, he wanted to defend his position: "Since the exile, Israel has not killed any more prophets." All the others seemed to agree with him. But to Jesus it was as if a veil covered them, so that they saw but did not perceive, they heard but did not understand (Isa. 6:9). He had to uncover the dark power that prevailed under a seemingly harmless exterior among the people.

> *You know that Herod is a welcome guest among the rich people of Galilee. Not long ago he invited many of the distinguished people to a feast. At that feast he was seduced by the dance of a beautiful young girl and in his blindness had the Baptizer executed. All the respected people of Galilee were there, the court officials, the officers, and the distinguished citizens; all saw the murderous injustice and no one had the courage to stand up against it. Didn't all of them*

become implicated in the crime, and doesn't blood cleave to the hem
of their garments (Jer. 2:34)? Israel has slain a prophet.

All of them remembered the terrible deed that had enraged them too.
But in that connection they had never thought about a complicity of
the guests, nor even less about a crime committed by Israel. Throughout Galilee they were only accusing Herodias, Herod's devilish wife,
because she had goaded him to kill the Baptist.

There was a Pharisee among those who heard him. He wanted to
defend Israel against Jesus. "The ruler had a wicked father and he
was seduced by an adulteress. The prominent people who were at the
feast could do nothing to rectify that breaking of the Torah and they
themselves condemned it in their own homes. Why should the blood
of John cleave to Israel?" This objection was intended sincerely. But
did it come out of a deceitful mouth which spoke of peace where
ambush was planned (Jer. 9:8)? Jesus began once more:

You have heard that some years ago the Roman governor had men
from Galilee massacred by the sacrifice in the Temple. So it was that
their blood was mixed with that of the sacrificial animals. Why
did the disaster strike precisely these men? Do you think that the
murdered Galileans were greater sinners than the other pilgrims
and the inhabitants of Jerusalem? No, they had even distinguished
themselves by their zeal for Israel and the Torah of Moses. Their ill
fate is rather a sign of the truth of prophetic words.

> **There is no faithfulness and loving-kindness,**
> **no knowledge of God in the land.**
> **No, there is swearing and lying,**
> **killing, robbery, and adultery.**
> **They break all bounds,**
> **and murder follows murder. (Hos. 4:1–2)**

Many were deeply affected by this voice of Hosea. However, some
of them rebelled against the way Jesus related the words of the
prophets to the present. They thought among themselves, "We would

never have slain the prophets if we had lived in their days." But their only response to him was a cold silence. He said for the last time, *You complain with all Israel because of oppression by the Roman government. Can't you see and confess that by this oppression a judgment on Israel has been decreed? Everyone needs to repent!*

God's Wrath and the Snare of Evildoers

Where the forces of death rule, extending a net of deception and camouflage over themselves, the glory and freedom of God cannot abide with human beings. Jesus perceived with growing intensity the powers that opposed the work of his Father and his message. While he was suffering from this unbridgeable opposition, words of judgment came involuntarily to his lips. He didn't yet have a good sense of its ultimate extent, but he certainly felt that images of wrath were forced upon him, and he knew with unshakable clarity that those who closed themselves to the word would not find salvation. Would his Father likewise change his countenance toward these sinners and come upon them in wrath?

Among the woman who accompanied him was Mary Magdalene. She spoke little but was always close to him when he spoke and she listened with an open heart. She drank in thoroughly the words of the one who had healed her. In a world full of spiritual lethargy, full of inner weariness and distrust, her readiness to hear and her undivided love touched him deeply. A short while before, with contorted face and disheveled hair, she had been under the spell of demonic powers; but now a deep peace lay on her when she listened to the words of the kingdom of God. What was it about the forces of the evil one that they could have so completely entrapped a heart which was so open to his Father? Where did the evil one lead those people who could not be won for the kingdom?

The contrast between the dark resistance of Israel and the loving openness of a given person's heart, which until a short time ago was addicted to the demonic forces, brought home to him the peculiar character of evil. Mary Magdalene sat close to him without interrupting him through word or gesture as he thought through the unlighted ways on which people became lost. He let his mind be taken over by the recollection of those Pharisees and scribes who had confronted him in such a hostile manner, and at the same time he allowed his spirit to be flooded with many passages and images from Holy Scripture, which accompanied him on his journey through the dark world.

> **If the wicked person does not repent**
> **he sharpens his sword,**
> **he bends and strings his bow.**
> **He prepares his deadly weapons,**
> **makes ready his fiery arrows.**
> **He makes a pit, digging it out,**
> **and falls into the pit he himself has made.**
> **His crime comes upon his own head,**
> **on the top of his head his violence falls back.**
>
> (Ps. 7:13, 15–16)

This was exactly what happened to Judah and Samaria. Like two shameless sisters they had sold themselves to the mighty Assyrians and Babylonians. But it was by just these lovers that both prostitutes were brought to disaster. Those very lords and riders, proud and arrogant on their steeds, with whom Judah and Samaria played the harlot, became the Lord's judgment upon them (Ezek. 23). The Egyptians in the days of Moses had to suffer a similar fate. Because they had revered vermin and wretched bugs, hordes of senseless animals came into their land, and they were obliged to learn that

> **one is punished by the very things with which one sins.**
>
> (Wisd. 11:16)

The very works of idolaters became their own destruction. They let themselves become anxious and afraid of those scarecrows in the cucumber field (Jer. 10:5) which their wicked, depraved hearts (Ps.

64:5–6) had created, and the gods burrowed their fearful faces into
the souls of those who made them (Ps. 135:18). Through their delu-
sion the idolaters bound themselves with chains, like the Egyptians
whose dark night arose out of their own hearts.

> Truly that night was without violence in itself;
> but out of the depths of powerless Hades it beset them,
> and they all slept the same sleep,
> but were driven by monstrous specters,
> and now were paralyzed by their souls' surrender,
> for sudden and unexpected fear overwhelmed them....
> For the whole world was illumined with brilliant light,
> and was engaged in unhindered work,
> while over those people alone heavy night was spread,
> an image of the darkness that was destined to receive them;
> but still heavier than darkness were they to themselves.
> (Wisd. 17:14–15, 20–21)

The darkness that was destined to receive them? Babylon, in the
arrogance of its heart, wanted to climb up to heaven and establish its
throne over the stars of God (Isa. 14:13–14). But the shining son
of dawn was thrown from heaven and plunged to earth. He presumed to rise up over the clouds but fell into the underworld, into the
lowest depth (Isa. 14:12–15). There the rulers and realms he had vio-
lated were ready for him with humiliation and torment. Likewise the
daughters of the Chaldeans had to undergo their humiliation with exposed genitals (Isa. 47:2–3), and their dead were lying on the ground
despised and without burial (Isa. 14:19). The same catastrophe struck
her that had come upon Israel, for she was arrogant, thinking "I am
and there is no one besides me" (Isa. 47:8). So a dark veil lay over all
the nations (Isa. 25:7), and for the idolaters all creatures and aspects
of creation, whose praise of the Creator they would not hear, became
terror and judgment.

Also the chosen people ran after false gods and followed the evil
impulse of its heart (Jer. 16:12). Even Solomon served alien gods

(1 Kings 11:5–8), and many prophets proclaimed visions which arose out of their own imagination (Jer. 23:16). From guilt and anxiety the people saw their God in the mirror and in the visions of their own corrupt hearts, and this obscured the countenance of Yahweh so much that prayer could no longer pass through the clouds to him (Lam. 3:44).

Jesus felt as if he himself was passing into the innermost life of the unfaithful nation. The presence of his Abba receded, and he saw a fearsome being over him which blazed in mighty wrath from heaven (Jer. 15:14), spewed consuming fire (Joel 2:3), and devoured everything around it and aimlessly destroyed (Ezek. 21:9–10). It became clear to him all of a sudden — the unfaithful people had been able to perceive its God still only in this frightful face. The prophets were constrained to proclaim the character of God as it came to be understood by a rebellious, corrupt, and violent city. The princes, priests, and false prophets, because of the way they conducted their affairs, could not even see this image of wrath (Zeph. 3:1–4). They had hidden themselves from the presence of the Lord (Gen. 3:8–10) in a twofold manner — concealing the wrath of God through a nationalistic ideology, which in turn projected divine wrath against other peoples.

After a long course through the world of evil, Jesus returned suddenly to the present. At first he felt dazed. Yet the flowers and trees about him and the mountains and clouds over him were rich with colors. He took a deep breath. A many-voiced singing moved in the warm air, and he heard deep in his ear a fine and gentle playing. All things about him praised their Creator. The grimaces of the idols and the images of anxieties and chains fell away from him, and the freedom and wisdom of God played for him on the entire earth (Prov. 8:31). Mary Magdalene, whose loving heart and dark past had invited him to explore the world of evil, was still sitting nearby. She had accompanied him with great concern; however, she did not disturb his inner journey with even a word.

By the Measure of One's Own Heart

In the villages beyond the lake and to the east of the Jordan crowds of people flocked around as soon as Jesus appeared. He healed the sick, spoke in parables, and often in his speaking the dark world of the lost emerged. Pharisees and scribes said to each other, "When Moses performed signs before Pharaoh by the command of God, the Egyptian diviners were also able, with the help of demons, to work miracles. But in competition with the great deeds of Moses, the evil spirits failed." They decided therefore to test Jesus and demanded — like the tempter in the wilderness — a great sign in which they could learn the full extent of his power. His rejoinder to them:

> *Remember how in the time of Jonah Nineveh repented. What sign did the mighty pagan city have for its conversion? None other than the preaching of the prophet. For the kingdom of God likewise: if you had heard the message with open hearts, then you would recognize the power by which I have spoken.*

The disciples too had for a long time secretly awaited an overwhelming miracle by which the opposition to their master would be broken. When the Pharisees and scribes confronted him with their demand, they had hoped that he would take it up and reduce them to silence once and for all with a wonderful mighty deed. Jesus saw through their thoughts and said to them after the Pharisees had gone away: *By the measure with which one measures will it be measured out to you.* They didn't understand what he wanted to tell them and what his words had to do with the miracle for which they waited. He explained to them,

> *All of us carry in our heart a measure by which we measure and judge whatever we encounter. Whoever is full of mistrust sees everything in light of his suspicion, and the greater the mighty deeds of God that he meets, the more demonic he will interpret them to be. The Son of Man has driven out demons. Many Pharisees and scribes, however, bear suspicion in their hearts and assert that the*

Son of Man has formed a covenant with Beelzebul, the prince of demons.

The disciples remembered vividly the wicked words against their master and they felt simultaneously the degree to which they had entered into a world which was scarcely comprehensible to them.

In a village they were passing through Jesus told the people flocking around him a parable.

A wealthy man went on a long journey. Before he left he summoned his servants to him and entrusted them with all his wealth and, indeed, to each one according to his ability. To the first one he gave five talents of gold, to the next two talents, and to the third one talent. Then he took his leave; but the servants acted according to their respective characters. After quite a long time, the lord returned. The first two servants, who meanwhile had doubled the entrusted amount, were treated kindly at the settling of accounts, according to the faithfulness of their hearts. To the total that had been placed in their care the master added the number of talents they earned for him. But the third servant said to the proprietor, "Here is your money. I hid it while you were gone, for you are a severe man and harvest even though you have not sowed." The lord answered, "According to your own words and by the measure of your own heart the judgment falls on you. If you knew that I am so severe, why did you not take my money to the bank? I could have increased it then with the interest." Then he said to the other servants, "Take the one talent from him and give it to the one who already has ten." And he had the distrustful servant thrown out into outer darkness.

This parable disturbed the disciples. The tale offended most of them, and they didn't know what Jesus was trying to tell them. One expressed his displeasure: "The lord acted unjustly. The third servant had done nothing wicked, nevertheless the money was taken from him and given to the one who already possessed in abundance." Many thought similarly. Others didn't understand how the master, who at first seemed so kindly, had suddenly become so hardhearted. Jesus observed what they were thinking and said,

> *You find it hard to understand the lord in the parable. Yet how will you grasp the goodness and judgment of God? Why do you focus only on the money and not on the hearts in which everything is decided and in which the countenance of God is reflected?*

The listeners looked at him confusedly, but he continued:

> *Because of their faithfulness and trust the first two servants found a kindly lord. Because of his anxiety and distrust the third servant confronted a severe judge. Their hearts decided how the lord could present himself to them. Whoever has and believes will be ready to receive without limits. Whoever bears suspicion in his heart, his distrust undermines what he already has.*

A great murmuring followed these words, and in small groups they were further debated. Some thought Jesus was speaking more and more incomprehensibly. Others concluded still that the lord in the parable had acted unjustly. Still others wondered how it was that one's own heart could change the lord. Jesus saw their lack of understanding and exclaimed in the kind of language they understood, *Sinners will be cast into hell where the fire is never extinguished.* They were shocked. Jesus, however, wondered how the goodness of his Father could reach those who had paralyzed and enclosed themselves in their own world. He lived in the light of his Father and was biding his time concerning the world of the lost. The tension within him grew.

In Search of the Lost

One day the disciples asked if all enemies would be destroyed with the coming of the kingdom of God. So they understood it from the prophets. Jesus sensed their impatience and their wish that the conflicts into which they had been drawn with the Pharisees and scribes might soon be triumphantly concluded. He didn't give them a direct answer, for much was indeed unclear to him. He told them, however, a parable:

> *A shepherd had one hundred sheep. When he counted them as usual he found that one was missing. So he left the ninety-nine and took as long as it required in the search, until the lost sheep was found. With joy he put it on his shoulders and carried it home. At home he called his friends and neighbors and invited them to a feast.*

The disciples were puzzled by the parable, but took note that it disappointed their expectation of destruction of enemies. They talked about what he could have meant with the lost sheep, which was the object of so much attention and care. Was it those who had been with them and then separated from them? Surely Jesus couldn't have meant his enemies?

In the villages beyond the Jordan there were, along with Jews who kept the Torah, ones who hardly troubled themselves with the Torah of Moses. Here there were also numerous gentiles. In the places where he spent time Jesus spoke to everyone and even accepted invitations to eat with unobservant Jews. Scribes and Pharisees were indignant over this and demanded of him, "Who shares the blessing of the table with the godless, is that one not himself godless?" Jesus did not respond directly, but recounted also to them a parable:

> *A woman having ten gold pieces lost one of them. She lighted a lamp, swept the entire house and searched until she found the dinar. Then she went to her friends and invited them: come, we will celebrate and rejoice because I have found again what was lost.*

The Pharisees and scribes had followed his tale with distrustful faces. They could find no clear meaning in it. When he had finished, they said among themselves that he had avoided their question.

An unhoped for opportunity to test Jesus presented itself. In a larger group they came to him, already anticipating their triumph; their servants were dragging a woman who was trembling with fear.

They shoved her in front of them as a circle formed around him. Someone said, "This woman has been caught in the act of adultery. Moses prescribed in the Torah to stone such women. What do you say about her?" All listened for the answer as if waiting in ambush (Ps. 17:12). This time he wouldn't escape from them. If he spoke against stoning her, then they could accuse him of being an enemy of the Torah. If he agreed to the stoning, then his severe judgment would fall upon misunderstanding among the people and they would turn away from him. Jesus saw through their plot. He knew well that the Pharisees had customary ways of avoiding the penalty of death provided in the Torah. He looked first of all into their hostile faces and then he bent down and began to write with his finger in the dust (Jer. 17:13): **There is none that does good; no, not one** (Ps. 14:3). The Pharisees glanced at his signs on the ground and pressed him to give a clear answer. Then he straightened up and said, *Whoever among you is without sin, let him throw the first stone at her.* Immediately then he bent down again to write again. Those addressed were confused in the extreme, for no one had reckoned on this answer. After a moment of embarrassment the eldest among them moved away and all the others followed him. When the women was left by herself with Jesus and his disciples, he looked up. *Has no one condemned you?* She answered, "No one, lord." Then he imparted to her peace and comfort: *Neither do I condemn you. Go and sin no more.*

As she went away and her fear held in check burst forth in her tears, Jesus asked himself what he would have done if one of her accusers had been so blind as to throw the first stone at her. Then all would have imitated the first person. Would he have put himself in front of the woman to protect her from the lying and murderous gang? The experience he had in his home village appeared again before his inner eye, and he remembered the psalms in which the one praying implored to be rescued from deceitful, violent enemies. Would he come into a similar situation on his way to seek out those who were lost?

Most of the Pharisees and scribes were furious that he had escaped their trap. Some of them, however, were becoming more uncertain in their hearts and sought further to fathom the confusing teaching and odd behavior of the preacher from Nazareth. Why was he now severely demanding and now incomprehensibly compassionate? One of them ventured to test Jesus again. He asked, "May a man dismiss his wife because of her adultery?" Instead of an answer Jesus gave him back a question: *What did Moses write for you?* The scribe replied, "He allowed us to issue a certificate of divorce and to dismiss the woman" (Deut. 24:1). Jesus agreed with him and led him further into the matter at the same time. *Yes, so it stands written. But you haven't related everything that Moses taught.* The scribe was honestly taken aback and asked, stunned, what else was written in the Torah about divorce. Jesus answered him,

> *Have you not read that in the beginning of the creation God created man and woman* (Gen. 1:27).

> **Therefore a man leaves father and mother and cleaves to his wife, and they shall become one flesh.** (Gen. 2:24)

> *Since they are one, man shall not separate what God has bound.*

The scribe was confused. "But Moses himself, who taught us about the creation of man and woman, permitted divorce." Jesus waited some time, and then he began as if he would speak of something else:

> *Since the first sin a deep darkness lies on human beings, and their hearts are hardened. Even the Torah participates in this dark world, and it's only for this reason that Moses permitted divorce. Learn to distinguish between God's original will and what the Lord conceded to you through Moses because of your obstinacy and hardheartedness.*

The disciples were just as surprised by these words as the scribe. They had never seen the commands of Moses in this way. When they were alone with him they implored him, "Teach us the original will of God for human beings." He turned to them in love in order to implant a deep picture in their hearts.

In the union of man and woman the will of God has appeared since the beginning of creation. It was the same intention for which he called Abraham, Isaac, and Jacob, and he chose their descendants for himself, as a bridegroom chooses his bride (Isa. 62:5). In a covenant of everlasting love he united with his bride (Ezek. 16:10–14). But the chosen one abandoned herself to her own beauty. She became unfaithful to her husband, played the harlot, and became a prostitute (Ezek. 16:15–63). Will the chosen one now be disowned? No, God is not like a human (Hos. 11:9). He remembers his everlasting covenant and his intention from the beginning, and he will seek the lost until he finds them. Then he will celebrate a great festival of joy.

These words fell like dew on the souls of the disciples, although there was much they still could not understand. They noticed that he gave allusions to parables they hadn't understood, and they started to get an intimation of something new.

Out of the Pit of Dread into the Light

Jesus let himself be led by the words of the prophets, and they posed new questions for him. How could the Messiah reach the lost whose hearts resisted the word of his Father? Would the Spirit that came upon him enable him to heal them?

> **The Spirit of the Lord shall rest upon him,**
> **the Spirit of knowledge and fear of God. . . .**
> **With righteousness he judges the helpless**
> **and arbitrates for the poor of the land.**
> **And he shall smite the earth with the rod of his mouth,**
> **and with the breath of his lips he shall slay the wicked.**
>   (Isa. 11:2, 4)

He himself had struck the hardhearted with the word of his mouth in order to wake them, but not to slay them. His way must be different from the one given in Isaiah's oracle. Didn't Scripture itself indicate the true way? It spoke of God circumcising the hearts of sinners (Deut. 30:6), placing his Spirit within them, and changing hearts of stone into hearts of flesh (Ezek. 36:26). Yet how could this miracle come about after the word of forgiveness had rebounded off a wall of indifference and rigidity? Was there a way to gain access to people who were caught in the spell of the dark power and whose hearts remained imprisoned?

Jesus decided to separate himself from his disciples and the women who followed him so as to listen without interference to the voice of his Father. He took with him only Simon and the two sons of thunder, James and John. While they slowly approached a tall mountain, he walked alone most of the time and thought about the fate of those who had been sent to Israel before him. The people had murmured against Moses and banded together against him. Likewise David, in many of his songs, complained that lying evildoers surrounded him in ambush. Were these not signs that the Messiah, the shoot out of Jesse's stump (Isa. 11:1), must follow a similar path? He saw the contorted faces of the possessed before him and perceived in their features all of Israel, while the memory of his journey through the world of the evil one rose up within him again. Yet simultaneously the tender power of his Father pressed upon him to seek after the unfortunate even into their final loneliness and the dungeons of their souls. Then it struck him that he had spoken to himself, without conscious intention, lines from a psalm:

> He drew me out of the pit of dread,
> out of the slime and mire.
> He put a new song in my mouth,
> a song of praise to our God.
> > (Ps. 40:2–3)

He stopped suddenly, for a thought seized him: would he himself fall into such a pit of horror, into slime and mire, when he went seeking the lost?

When Jesus arrived at the top of the mountain with his three disciples, they saw the entire land before them, from Gilead as far as Dan and from Naphtali over Ephraim and Manasseh as far as Judah (Deut. 34:1–2). A thunderstorm broke loose and claps of thunder seemed to tear the mountain (1 Kings 19:11). While wind and storm raged, Jesus prayed to his Abba for the salvation of his people, whom he perceived to be in deep darkness. Slowly he recited psalms, songs of his people, and while he prayed he himself slid into the words that came upon his lips. His self was at one with his people (Ps. 2), and he experienced with body and soul what the holy hymns expressed, as the form of the Son of Man disappeared from him. Evildoers and lying foes rose up, ganged up against him (Ps. 2:2–3), set snares for him (Ps. 140:5), and made an attempt on his life (Ps. 38:12). He was struck down, fell into a deep pit (Ps. 69:15). Waves and billows crashed over him (Ps. 42:7). Then the bars of the earth were closed (Jon. 2:6), and dread encompassed him (Isa. 24:17–18), a black night of terror.

Suddenly, however, a space above him opened; a hand drew him out of the snares of death, a breath of new life was breathed into him, and a voice full of indescribable blessing spoke: **This is my beloved son in whom I am well pleased.** He had gone the way of the Son of Man. His soul was as a bird escaped from the net of the hunter (Ps. 124:6), and it knew that it had gone yet deeper in the journey through darkness with the Son of Man. A stream of light transformed and transfigured him, and a new luster fell on the Scriptures of Moses and the prophets, which he had long known. Then all of a sudden Moses and Elijah appeared before him, and they concurred with what he had experienced. All the Scriptures showed him now that the Messiah must seek out the chosen people and those who are lost in their deepest need and distress in order to lead them to salvation and glory.

The three disciples, Simon, John, and James, were so terrified through the storm that they fell to the ground. As the sun broke through again, they observed in Jesus, who had remained standing near them, a profound change. The skin of his face radiated light (Exod. 34:30), and he seemed to float away from them. What had happened to him? A shining cloud floated past (Num. 9:15) and figures appeared. They heard a voice, which deeply bewildered them. They wanted to speak, but Simon could come up with only incoherent words. Great dread seized all three, and trembling they hid their faces. The time escaped them, until they heard someone calling to them: *Stand up, have no fear!* They ventured to raise their heads and they saw Jesus alone.

On the way back down he spoke to them in confidence and trust: *The Son of Man will be persecuted and delivered into the hands of his enemies. God, however, will deliver him from the violence of the evildoers and the evil powers.* Simon had again taken courage, and he was ashamed of the fear that had befallen him on the mountain. Now he wanted to demonstrate his new courage. He drew up to Jesus and whispered urgently to him, "God will protect you and deliver you from your enemies." He hoped for praise, but he was struck with embarrassment and anxiety to hear: *Get away from me, tempter. You are a stumbling-block to me, for you don't seek what God wills, but speak like all other men.* Deeply perplexed, Simon wondered whether Jesus had addressed the harsh words to him or was actually speaking to some other who was also there. Were there powers which secretly followed him? In what world was he? Simon didn't dare ask another question, and they were all silent the rest of the way.

As Jesus approached the place where he had left the other disciples, he saw from a distance a great crowd of people. He heard shouts and cries, and he felt with his entire body how difficult and burdensome this people had become for him. He had often seen how the mood could suddenly tilt from one extreme to the other and shift from enthusiasm to rejection. However, he had never been able to have the experience of seeing that his word touched the hearts of every individual in a great throng and brought them together in a new community of brothers and sisters. So he slowed his step and would have liked to turn around to pass the time undisturbed in the mysterious peace granted to him on the mountain. Even in the healings strength always flowed out of him, and scarcely ever did it return to him. He had given and burned himself out. A deep fatigue overcame him. But at the same time he felt compelled to depart for Jerusalem; since the experience on the mountain he knew even more clearly that the last task would await him there.

It wasn't long until the crowd at the edge of the village noticed his arrival from a distance. They all set off and hurried toward him. The first people to reach him spoke rapidly in confusion. The disciples weren't able to heal the boy; Pharisees made fun of them; the possessed man was going berserk; was Jesus stronger than the unclean spirit? In the crowd that followed him a man pushed his way to the front whose face was deeply anguished. A group followed him who held fast a youth in their midst. When the man with a tormented visage stood before Jesus the circle closed about them, and the distressed man implored him: "Master, help my son, as he is my only one." Jesus asked what was the matter with him. Out of the crowd several shouted pell-mell that the boy was possessed by a mute spirit and he gnashed his teeth. Often foam came out of his mouth, as with an animal, and he rolled about on the ground and fell into water. Jesus looked at those around them. He could sense nothing of trust; but he saw in the eyes of many a burning curiosity about what would happen now. He could not and would not give in to this desire and called in a loud voice to the crowd, *You unbelievers, how long must I bear your hardened hearts?* The crowd was dumbfounded by the rebuke and fell silent. But at this moment the boy tore away from the men who had led him there, fell on the ground, and rolled in the dust. Foam appeared on his lips. Jesus, moved, asked the father, *How long has he been like this?* He answered, "From childhood on. The evil spirit has even tried to kill him. He has often thrown himself into water or fire, and we have had a struggle to rescue him. He suffers, and we suffer with him. If you can, have compassion on us and help us!"

The double distress, of the youth and of his family, touched Jesus profoundly and he replied to the father, *You ask whether I can help. What you hope for doesn't come from a wonderworker at whom a throng stares. But for God anything is possible, and whoever trusts him with his whole heart can do anything. Do you believe?* The question struck the man's heart and he felt as though he was lifted up out of the crowd. In his need and helplessness he cried out, without rightly knowing what he said, "I believe, help my unbelief!" In this cry Jesus felt a soul that in its despair let all calculation and self-security fall away. It was the cry of a tormented creature who no longer hoped for deliverance. Jesus took his misery to heart and it became his own. He felt in himself a tremendous powerlessness: he gave himself to it and released his will to it. While he turned himself completely over to his Abba he was pulled into a dark pit.

But then a stream of power and confidence suddenly rose up in him and he saw the youth who was still rolling before him on the ground. As to an invisible force he spoke: *You deaf and dumb spirit, leave the boy and come back no more!* Then it cried out the way a crowd would shout: "We are legions." Jesus only repeated, *Come out!* The boy reared up and once more yelled out. Yet this time it was evident that the lad himself had cried out. He fell back on the ground and remained lying there motionless. The real outcry of the boy, who heretofore had only pressed his lips tightly together and gnashed his teeth, affected the people to the core. There were uncanny sounds, which at the same time resounded back to them like the echo of their own cries. Frightened, the crowd moved back from the youth. Quickly, however, they were pushing forward again and saying to each other that the lad was dead. Jesus bent down, took the motionless boy by the hand, and he stood up — shaking and exhausted. As he stammered his first words, Jesus returned him to his father. They embraced each other crying and sobbing, and so their long and unbearable anxiety began to leave them. When the bystanders pressed forward to touch the youth, Jesus used the curiosity occasioned by the healing to depart. His disciples followed him, rejoicing that the Pharisees, who had ridiculed them, had been silenced and that the people no longer heeded them, but were altogether preoccupied with the healed youth.

In a grove with many olive trees Jesus passed the remainder of the day. The disciples drew back while he rested under a tree (Gen. 18:4). Some went into the village to buy bread and fish; others got water. Before it became dark they started a small fire on which the women prepared the fish. When the meal was ready, Jesus came to the ones who were his own and accepted something to eat. As soon as he ate,

they felt more free and began to speak ardently about the events of the
day. They told Jesus they themselves had commanded the evil spirit to
come out. But from the boy came only a noise like a devilish laugh,
and he had only gnashed his teeth all the more. Some Pharisees in
the crowd had said triumphantly that now all would see what kind of
power they had. They also reviled Jesus and asserted that he was in
league with Satan. When they tried to defend him, the Pharisees only
laughed them to scorn. The Pharisees said they were only uneducated
people, could understand nothing of the Torah, and had let themselves be seduced by an impostor. Judas was quite aroused in anger as
he reported on these rebukes. Jesus was struck by this anger, and he
looked at him full of concern.

The others asked why they couldn't expel the demons. During their
first preaching trip many evil spirits had fled from them. Jesus asked
in return: *Did you pray without ceasing and thank the Father for his
work?* Their heads sank in embarrassment. Jesus didn't let a painful silence prevail, but immediately continued speaking: *There are evil forces
which only flee from a heart that is constantly united with the Father in
heaven. They can be driven out only through prayer.* All were silent. Andrew, who in contrast to his brother Simon preferred to listen when
others spoke, interrupted the silence. "When the others tried to heal
the youth I prayed silently to God for success, so that the Pharisees
could not defeat you and us. But in spite of that, the evil spirit was
not driven out and only laughed."

Great disappointment echoed in the voice of Andrew, which called
forth in the others that puzzlement and perplexity into which they
had been cast by the Pharisees before the return of their master. Jesus
felt their growing despondency and said, *God is not powerless, but your
faith is weak.* He sought to make it clear to them, for he remembered
the feeling of powerlessness regarding the misery of the possessed boy
himself.

*Faith is mighty, and nevertheless it is not a weapon to achieve
victory over others. It is quite small and yet it brings forth great
things. If your faith were only like a mustard seed and you were to*

say to a mountain, "Be moved away from here!" it would happen,
for nothing is impossible for God and faith in God.

Some disciples cheered up noticeably. Thomas asked, however, "How can we achieve a faith which can move mountains?" Jesus left them to their own thoughts for a few moments. Then he began to tell them a parable:

> *In a certain city there lived a judge who neither feared God nor troubled himself about a reputation for righteousness among men. In the same city lived an impoverished widow, whom a dishonest relative had robbed of all her goods. She went unceasingly to the judge, begging him to obtain justice for her against the enemy among her own relatives. Because she could not bribe the judge with money, he kept ordering her away for a long time. However, the widow didn't give up. Finally the judge said, "I will have to trouble myself with her case; otherwise she will make a scene with me in public and even slap me in the face. That would be disgraceful for me."*

Once more Jesus let them think their own thoughts. However, when he saw their questioning faces, he drew the teaching out of his story for them. *If a dishonest judge may be moved by stubborn pleading, won't the Father in heaven help that person who trusts him day and night like a child?*

Among the followers who listened to him and dreamed of power were certain women. In the light of the fire, which was burning ever lower, he took notice of the face of Mary Magdalene: it was utterly open and drank in each of his words. Would she pray day and night? And Judas, who got so worked up? The disciple from Kirioth was now quite preoccupied and seemed to be caught up in very serious thoughts.

Late in the evening the north wind came up and blew through the grove (Song 4:16). They all covered themselves in their cloaks. Toward morning as the first light showed itself in the east, Jesus got up. He went out of the grove toward the sunrise. Mary Magdalene followed him after a short time. Away from the grove she became frightened, as she could no longer see him and some men came to a nearby field (Song 3:1). But then she saw that he entered a vineyard close by on a hill, and she hurried along the same path. Dew lay on the grass and the night dripped from the shrubs and trees (Song 5:2). The disciples unwrapped themselves likewise from their cloaks, stood up, and went into the fields toward the dawn. As the sun came up over the hill, they saw Jesus standing above. Light enwrapped him and rays of light surrounded him (Hab. 3:4). Their souls were stolen away by this sight (Song 6:12).

Israel's Hard-Heartedness and the Feast for the Pagans

As they started out for Jerusalem they were all full of expectation. The teaching about faith that could move mountains had given them new strength. Most of them were hoping that their master would there announce the messianic kingdom and by his faith remove all hindrances. They even began to dispute with one another about who would be the greatest in the coming kingdom. Simon, who had already forgotten again the scolding from Jesus when they descended from the mountain, participated heatedly. Also James and John asserted themselves. The mother of these two, who was with the women, even took both her sons, approached Jesus, and fell at his feet with the plea, "Promise that my sons will sit beside you on your right and your left in your kingdom." Amazed, Jesus looked at all three and replied, *You know not what you ask. Are you able to drink the cup of dread and suffering?* Both brothers answered, full of zeal but without really knowing what they said: "We are able." Jesus responded, lost in thought, yet firmly, *My Father will grant it to you, but his ways are other than you think. Only he has the authority to allot positions in his kingdom.*

The other disciples, following this whole thing, were angry at the woman and her two sons. Why should they have preeminence? Simon hoped to have the top rank for himself, and likewise the others certainly didn't want to have inferior positions. Jesus acted for some time as though he didn't notice the argument among his disciples. But then he waved a child to him, took it in his arms, and said to the disciples, *If you don't give up your will to rule, there will be no place for you in the realm of my Father. Only whoever is as little as this child here will be great before my Father.* The disciples, ashamed and embarrassed, said nothing. Jesus continued: *See this child, how it looks at the world with open eyes! It is all eyes and ears and completely forgets itself. Only when you look at the Father like this, obey his will, and forget your own desires, will his kingdom come to you. Do you want to travel the way with me on which he leads us?* Relieved, they agreed enthusiastically and were happy he had dropped the subject of their dispute.

As they journeyed they talked about the messianic time. Some of them remembered having heard from the learned in Scripture that Elijah would return. So they asked Jesus whether this prophet, who was taken up to heaven in a chariot of fire, would come back on the earth. He answered by citing the words of the prophet Malachi:

> **Behold, I will send you Elijah**
> **before the great and terrible day of the Lord comes.**
> **He will turn the hearts of the fathers to their sons**
> **and the hearts of the sons to their fathers,**
> **lest I come and devote the land to destruction.**
>
> (Mal. 4:5–6)

When they demanded of him when this would happen, they were surprised by his answer: *Elijah has already come and preached. People listened to him for only a short while and then did with him as they pleased and killed him. Will something similar happen to the Son of Man?* The disciples didn't understand whom he meant by Elijah. A few assumed he was alluding to John the Baptist. Others were of the view that it was a parable, for the true Elijah could not be conquered by his foes. Indeed, the prophet called down fire from heaven and had all the priests of Baal executed at the brook Kishon (1 Kings 18:30–40). Against this someone broke in: "Scribes say that Elijah will return and be slain by blasphemers. But a short time thereafter the Messiah will appear and raise him up." Someone else said, "Will the murdered Baptist perhaps be resurrected when we enter Jerusalem with Jesus?" Most of them didn't know what to think. What they heard, however, gave them new food for thinking and dreaming.

When they crossed over the Jordan and came into the border area of Samaria, they wanted to spend the night in a village. But the Samaritans kept them out, as they wanted nothing to do with Galileans on their way to Jerusalem to worship in the Temple there. They followed their fathers in praying to God only on Mt. Gerezim, the mount of blessing, for there the tribes of Israel had been assembled after entering into the promised land in order to call down blessings upon the people and to hurl curses at all those who became unfaithful (Deut. 27:11–26). Some Samaritans had even presumed some decades before to scatter human bones in the sanctuary in Jerusalem. Since then the conflict had increased dangerously. James and John had gone on ahead and reported indignantly the refusal of the villagers. Since their heads were still full of thoughts about Elijah, they asked Jesus, "Should we command that fire from heaven fall on these evildoers?" Jesus reprimanded them sharply: *You don't know whose children you are. God makes his sun rise upon the good and the evil, and his steadfast love reaches as far as the clouds* (Ps. 57:10). *Learn from him and not from the desire for revenge, which belongs to sinners.*

When they came to Jericho, the city of palms (Deut. 34:3), a lush blooming filled the entire area of the oasis, although it was still early in the spring. The city lived out of the memory of the conquest: it was the first city in Canaan to be conquered after Joshua and the twelve tribes had crossed over the Jordan. The ancient memory awoke, however, no new life and no living faithfulness to the God of the ancestors. Now there were, above all, signs of wealth in the city, for trade routes met in the oasis and Herod had ordered the construction of baths and pools and great gardens.

Gilgal had once existed near there. There all the men of Israel had submitted to circumcision after the entry into the promised land, and there Joshua had had put in place twelve huge stones which the twelves tribes had brought with them from the bottom of the Jordan when they walked over the riverbed with dry feet (Josh. 4:1–24). Also there the prophets Elijah and Elisha had worked (2 Kings 2:1; 4:38). Yet no trace of Gilgal had remained, and its memorial signs must have suffered the same fate as Shiloh, which the Lord devoted to destruction because of the sins of Israel (Jer. 7:12).

Due to the brisk commerce there were many customs officials and tax collectors in Jericho. Zacchaeus, the chief of the customs officials, who had many collectors under him, had heard of the coming of Jesus and wished to see him. Since he was quite short and many of the people in the city crowded around Jesus, he ran on ahead and climbed up into a sycamore tree. When Jesus passed by, he stopped and looked up. He saw the man sitting above and recognized that he was a rich gentleman. What kind of interest would the distinguished man have in him that he put himself into such a strange, indeed even an almost painful position? He called to him: *Come down quickly! Today I must be your guest.* Zacchaeus was embarrassed when everyone looked up at him. Yet at the same time he was very happy that Jesus wanted to come to his home. As fast as he could he clambered down and took Jesus to his place. After the meal Zacchaeus said to his guest, "Your visit has deeply honored me, and I would like to become a new person. If I have defrauded anyone, I will give it back to him fourfold; also I will give away half my goods to the poor."

Many scribes from Jerusalem spent some time in the city of palms. Some of them had been among the populace witnessing the conversation at the sycamore tree. They had heard from Galilean sources much that was suspicious about Jesus. Now they were able to hear for themselves that he intended to be a guest of the head tax collector. How could he proclaim the kingdom of God and yet share the blessing of the table with a person who was not at all concerned with the divine Torah? They were indignant and agreed with the judgment that the community of Pharisees in Galilee had spoken against him.

Jesus was told how angry they were. When he happened to meet some of them, he said to them, *Salvation has come to the house of Zacchaeus because he too is a son of Abraham. Is it allowed to seek and redeem the lost?* They had nothing to reply. Then he broke out in indignation:

> *You scribes and Pharisees, hypocrites! You are zealous for inciden-*
> *tal things, you trouble yourselves to give a tithe on every spice*
> *or condiment, but the weightiest matters of the Torah you leave*
> *aside: righteousness and mercy. Blind leaders, all of you! With your*
> *judgments you strain out a gnat and swallow a camel.*

Some of these teachers of the Torah retorted angrily, "Master, you offend us by these words." Jesus asked in return,

> *Don't you yourselves speak your own judgment? Around Jerusalem*
> *you build tombs for the prophets whom your forebears murdered,*
> *and you announce noisily, "If we had lived in the days of our fa-*
> *thers we wouldn't have been guilty of the death of the prophets." So*
> *with that you admit that you are descendants of murderers of the*
> *prophets. And are you trying to show that you have improved over*
> *your fathers? You condemn the Son of Man who teaches righteous-*
> *ness and compassion. In so doing you follow exactly the way of your*
> *ancestors and judge with the criterion of murderers of the prophets.*
> *How do you expect to escape from hell?*

Most of the scribes and Pharisees turned away from him silently and in bitter indignation. One, however, who remained there asked, "Is the compassion you proclaim meant also for those without the Torah and pagans? Only Israel is God's vineyard (Isa. 5:1–7), and on the day of judgment the Lord will trample the peoples (Hab. 3:12) who are devoted to the nothingness of idols and who have troubled themselves only for the fire" (Jer. 51:58). His words represented the proud election-faith of Israel. Jesus asked him only,

> *Have you not read the prophets to see how often Israel is condemned.*
> *And don't you know the word of the Lord about the peoples?*

> **The Lord will make a feast on Zion,**
> **a feast for all peoples of fat things,**

> a feast of wine on the lees,
> of fat things full of marrow.
> And he will tear off the covering on this mountain
> that covers all nations,
> the veil that is spread over all peoples. (Isa. 25:6–7)

Yea, many will come from East and West and hold a feast of thanksgiving with Abraham, Isaac, and Jacob in the kingdom of my Father; but many who were initially appointed for the kingdom will be cast out into darkness.

The scribe replied, in angry agitation, "Do you still insist on teaching that the godless pagans will be preferred to Israel the chosen people?" Jesus said only, *If Israel returns to compassion it will also experience compassion.*

Cunning Cleverness and Simple Love

As they slowly walked up the steep and rocky road toward Jerusalem the disciples talked about the events in Jericho. The conversion of the chief tax collector had profoundly impressed them. However, Judas's attitude was cool. "Zacchaeus certainly doesn't know anymore which people he defrauded in the course of his life. All his wealth has come about due to dishonesty. Even if he now gives away half he's not doing a good deed, for the second half also, which he retains for himself, is the fruit of fraud." The others were astonished, with mouths hanging open. The beautiful picture that they had drawn of the conversion of Zacchaeus was suddenly tainted, and they became uncertain. Then Jesus intervened and told them a parable.

A rich man had a manager of his affairs, and he heard talk that the manager squandered the goods of his master. The master had him summoned and said to him, "What is this I'm hearing about you? Turn in an accounting! I can no longer entrust my goods to you." The manager was worried and considered how he could use the last few hours in his position to make friends for an uncertain future. He called the debtors to his lord to see him. To the first one, who owed for one hundred barrels of oil, he wrote a new note for fifty. For the second he lowered the debt from one hundred to eighty sacks of grain. So he did with everyone and this way he won many friends.

The disciples were even more confused by this parable. What did Jesus want to tell them with the story of a cheater? One gave his feelings loud expression: "The manager did a great wrong, for he embezzled someone else's goods." Jesus ignored the remark and began to praise the manager.

From his perspective he acted very cleverly, as he made friends for himself who would take care of him. Zacchaeus also was a clever man, because he made for himself friends with the money that he gave back to those he cheated or that he gave to the poor; these friends will intercede for him with God. Learn from his cleverness!

They were still perplexed. Observing this, Jesus began once more.

Think of Judith of Bethuliah, who became the glory of Israel and the pride of her people (Jud. 15:9). Without weapons, and clothed only with her seductive beauty, she went into the camp of the enemies to make her way with great cunning into the tent of Holofernes, the commander of the enemy. Thus she acted for the deliverance of Israel. Only the one who reaches by cleverness the innermost tent of the enemy camp can overcome the kingdom of the evil one. We're on the way toward that.

Judith in the camp of the enemy Assyrians and in the tent of Holofernes — this thrilled the spirit of the disciples, yet they still didn't understand what Jesus wanted to tell them.

On the way a Levite who was going up to the Temple had attached himself to them. He listened too, and the discourse about cleverness touched a sore point in his own quest. After the disciples had already been silent for a while, he ventured to say audibly, with a sigh, "The commandments are often difficult to understand." Jesus heard and turned to him with a question: *You know, don't you, the most important commands, to love God and neighbor?* "Of course," answered the Levite. "But who are my neighbors? Are they my relatives or even all members of our nation? The blasphemous Samaritans who desecrated the Temple or the godless pagans can certainly not be meant." Then he pointed down to the Dead Sea that was still visible in the distance, and he continued: "For the pious Essenes down there the neighbors are only those who live in their community. They keep their distance from the priests and Levites in Jerusalem and even refuse to offer sacrifices in the Temple, although they are prescribed in the Torah. It's sad, but there is conflict in Israel over the commandments of God, and it is hard to know who our neighbors are." Jesus sensed that his worry was authentic and deep. So he asked his disciples to stop for a rest and began to recount a parable to all who were with him.

A man was traveling alone on the steep and rocky road on which we're walking now. Suddenly he was attacked by thieves, struck down and robbed. He lay there half dead. After some time a priest came along, saw the wounded man lying at the edge of the road, and passed on by. A Levite did the same thing. Finally a Samaritan rode past. He had compassion, bound up his wounds, and set him on his own beast.

The Levite felt shocked that the half-pagan Samaritan was held before his eyes as a model. Jesus gave him a moment to ponder this, and then asked, *Which of these three do you think proved neighbor to the man who fell among thieves?* This question took the Levite aback a second time, and likewise the disciples, who had been listening. The disciples had expected another question: who was the neighbor of the three? This could only be the wounded man. But to the perplexing question as to who proved to be neighbor, the Levite answered after some hesitation and reflection: "The Samaritan." Jesus responded, *You have answered well. Now you yourself act as a neighbor on behalf of the poor and wounded. They will love you as themselves, and in this way you will learn to love them.*

The Judgment on Jerusalem and the World

On the day of their arrival in Bethany, where they had found shelter, Jesus climbed up the Mount of Olives with the twelve. The springlike warmth of Jericho gave way in the higher altitude to a cold wind from the north, which drove dark clouds before it. The holy city lay before them in a pale light. They stood silently for a long time viewing the Temple and its walls, which rose up over the Kidron Valley, while other pilgrims passed by them, singing.

> **Blessed those whom you choose and bring near,**
> **who dwell in your courts!**
> **We shall be satisfied with the goodness of your house,**
> **the good of your holy temple!** (Ps. 65:4)

When just for a minute the sun rays pierced through the clouds and fell on the Temple, the twelve broke out in loud astonishment. But suddenly they noticed that Jesus was crying. They hesitated, but finally asked him what distressed him. He looked steadily at the holy site and began to speak as if he were speaking only to the city.

> *If you had only known what brought you peace. But now it remains hidden from you. Your children have become obstinate and want to seek peace and freedom in their own name. But their deeds will only stir up powerful enemies, and complete misfortune will strike you. Armies will surround you and no stone will remain standing on the other.*

The twelve were deeply shocked when they heard this; they asked when this all would happen. Jesus answered: *The time of judgment has been shortened, but the exact hour lies in the hand of the Father.*

Meanwhile the sun's rays had disappeared and a storm whirled around them (Nahum 1:3). Jesus walked into the stiff wind, while the raging waters roared (Hab. 3:10). He called to the twelve: *Remember the word of the prophet Zechariah!*

> **I will gather all the nations to battle against Jerusalem. The city will be taken, the houses plundered, the women raped.... Yet the Lord will go forth.... On that day his feet will stand on the Mount of Olives which lies before Jerusalem on the east. The Mount of Olives will be split in the middle from east to west by a huge valley.** (Zech. 14:2, 4)

With these words a shudder shot through the bodies of the twelve. It was as if the ground had opened under their feet and an overpowering figure loomed over them. Without regarding their dread, Jesus went on:

> *People will quarrel with one another and nations do battle against each other. In those days a terrible storm will break out from the borders of the earth and the judgment will go forth from nation to nation. Many will hide in caves and in holes and in tombs* (1 Sam. 13:6). *The dead will lie from one end of the earth to the other. No one will lament; no one will gather and bury the dead* (Jer. 25:32–33).

The throats of the twelve tightened and they began to shake. While Jesus was speaking the storm had reached its full might, and he had to shout out the last words into the raging of the elements.

When it became somewhat calmer, he turned to the twelve: *The Lord God has handed over judgment to the Son of Man, and his word discloses how people and nations judge and condemn one another.* Then he moved with the freezing disciples to protection from the cold wind behind a wall, where they crouched down on the ground. After a long silence they heard once more the voice of Jesus, which had quite changed in the meantime. Its severity had turned into an infinite sad-

ness, and he began a lament over the beloved city and the peoples, as
once David had lamented over Saul and his friend Jonathan:

> Your glory, O Israel, is slain upon the high places.
> How are the heroes fallen!...
> You mountains of Gilboa,
> may no dew or rain fall upon you,
> you fields of offerings. (2 Sam. 1:19, 21)

After his lament had died away, he dismissed the twelve to return
to Bethany while he remained alone on the Mount of Olives. He suddenly saw himself on a mountain which grew ever higher and reached
into the clouds. He was becoming so united with the form of the
Son of Man that he now perceived himself completely within it and
looking back down at his human form. He looked into the depths of
heaven and earth (Ps. 113:6), and his eyes penetrated history, which
hastened on as the judgment of all peoples. The word proceeded from
his mouth as a two-edged sword through time and sharpened the
judgment.

A voice whispered to him, **With the breath of your lips you shall
slay the wicked** (Isa. 11:4). Yet this voice found no echo in his soul.
A boundless compassion for the victims of sin filled him. He wanted
to draw near to the many slain on the face of the earth and act as a
neighbor to them in order to share their fate in every way. As he saw
the multitude of the dead, he knew suddenly that he had to go with
them into death.

> The wicked lie in wait for the righteous
> and seek to slay them.
> The Lord will not abandon them to their hand,
> will not let them be condemned
> when they are brought to trial. (Ps. 37:32–33)

His Father would allow him to be condemned and cast into the pit of
horror. But he would draw him, with all the lonely and those struck
down, out of the jaws of death.

Third Act

Crucified as Victim of the Violent

Every year pilgrims streamed to Jerusalem for the Passover festival to commemorate there the liberation from the house of bondage, Egypt. Yet this time the remembering of the fate of the prophets was actually reenacted. The people of Anathoth and the inhabitants of Jerusalem had harbored plans to murder Jeremiah, who lived in the city like a trustful lamb (Jer. 11:18–23). He was persecuted because of his message. With him and many other prophets the Servant of the Lord was slain (Isa. 52:13–53:12). The people said (though this was piously deceptive) that God himself condemned him (Isa. 53:4). But what pierced him were the lying words and poisonous arrows of those who didn't recognize their own sins.

The number of pilgrims was great and far exceeded the inhabitants of the city. The pressure of crowds prevailed in the Temple and in the narrow streets, and the masses of people were excitable and volatile, so that merely a spark could spread among them to the point of riot. The Roman occupation force acted against actual or suspected instigators of disorder with brutal severity.

Jesus had to walk a tightrope in the city. Any deviation regarding the impending danger, no matter how wise it seemed, could betray the reign of God, whose fulfillment weighed on him more than ever. And any sort of bold behavior in the context of the religious and political excitement could quickly take the form of a suicidal provocation. Jesus resolved to give up all his own plans and all his concrete hopes for the sake of living only what the Father would show him from hour to hour through his inner voice and the signs that came to him. He let himself be led, trusting and innocent as a lamb, to the place of danger in order to do what his destiny demanded (1 Sam. 10:7).

The Messianic Entrance

As he started out the great images of judgment that had accompanied him since the arrival in Bethany no longer occupied him and a deep joy returned to him. It was the joy of the messianic age:

> **Rejoice greatly, O daughter of Zion!**
> **Shout for joy, O Jerusalem!**
> **Behold, your king comes to you.**
> **He is righteous and will deliver;**
> **he is humble and rides on an ass,**
> **on a colt the foal of an ass....**
> **He proclaims peace to the nations.**
> (Zech. 9:9–10)

All of a sudden he saw in the prophetic words a sign of the Father. On the Mount of Olives he sent two of his disciples into the nearest village to get a young donkey, while he, waiting for them, was absorbed in the view of the Temple and the city. All the disciples and women with him became eager and excited. Was this the moment for which they had been longing? Other pilgrims from Galilee, underway to the holy city, gathered on the Mount of Olives and caught the hope of the disciples. When the two who were sent came back with the donkey, some of them laid their garments on the humble beast, while others cut branches from the trees. They followed Jesus as he rode silently toward the city, as in a festal procession (Ps. 118:27), and they gave voice to the great thanksgiving and pilgrimage song:

> **Give thanks to the Lord, for he is good,**
> **for his steadfast love endures forever.**
> (Ps. 118:1)

With the final verses the crowd continued as if hanging on to them, and while they passed through the Kidron Valley under the east wall of the Temple they sang again and again the same words:

Hosanna! Blessed is he who comes in the name of the Lord.

(Ps. 118:26)

New groups of pilgrims attached themselves to them; the enthusiasm grew and many shouted, "Blessed be the reign of our father David, who now comes, and may Jerusalem be redeemed!"

Most of the disciples dreamed the longed for kingdom was about to come. But meanwhile completely different images were part of Jesus' understanding. While he was riding toward Zion he heard in the tops of the balsam trees the sound of marching steps (1 Chron. 14:15), and he saw violence and strife in the city of David (Ps. 55:9). The words from the pilgrimage song just sung stayed with him:

> **All nations surrounded me;**
> **I cut them off in the name of the Lord.**
> **They surrounded, surrounded me on every side;**
> **in the name of the Lord I cut them off. . . .**
> **The stone that the builders rejected**
> **has become the cornerstone.** (Ps. 118:10–11, 22)

A group of scribes and Pharisees was shocked to see the singing crowd. Did the false prophet from Galilee want to bring the messianic riot even into the holy city? They forced their way through to him and bombarded him with the demand to silence his blind followers. But Jesus seemed to be as if sunk into another world; he said only, *If they became silent, the very stones in the walls and the beams in the woodwork would cry out that much louder* (Hab. 2:11).

In the narrow side streets with a congestion of people the procession came to a halt. Jesus climbed off the donkey and had him taken back to the village where he had been untied. Immediately in the crowd he separated himself with some disciples from the other pilgrims who had accompanied him with their shouts. The messianic fire that briefly flared up was rapidly dying down in them as he walked inconspicuously through the city of David and climbed up slowly with his disciples around the circuit of Jerusalem (Neh. 12:27–43) to the Temple.

The Pool of Siloam lay close to the South Gate; there long ago the prophet Isaiah, with his son, had encountered King Ahaz to strengthen his faith regarding the enemy danger (Isa. 7:1–17). Because the people had then scorned trust in Yahweh, the gently flowing water of this pool, the huge and powerful waters of the Euphrates River — the Assyrian army — came in a flood over Israel, and they had almost washed away the holy city (Isa. 8:6–8). God let the raging nations sweep over his people as judgment. But precisely in this time of distress he came especially close to his chosen vineyard.

Through the little Tyropoeon Valley, built up with houses, the road led to the west up toward the upper city and Herod's palace. This ruler of foreign origin (on one side of his parentage) had never won the hearts of the Jews, and there were many stories of his bloody deeds. The people were amazed, however, at his great buildings and the Jerusalem Temple, which he had so forcefully and splendidly renovated. This man was a continual source of fascination and horror, although he was already long dead. When Jesus saw the palace of the tyrant and the towers he built, he said to his disciples: *Woe to him who bases his house on injustice and builds a city with blood. Every stone will be thrown down and the great wall will be laid bare. Cries of lament will fill the streets* (Mic. 1–3).

Between Herod's palace and the Temple mount the Citadel of the Maccabees rose up. Thereon hung that dark history which had begun with the endeavor to be faithful to the ancient traditions and soon had degenerated to a bloody struggle over political power. After the sword had been unsheathed in zeal for the Torah there was never peace again, for everything won by arms had to be defended by them. Judas Maccabeus fell in battle (1 Macc. 9:1–22), and his brother Jonathan allowed himself — in spite of his zeal for the Torah — to be appointed as high priest by a pagan king (1 Macc. 10:15–21), and he also was slain in battle (1 Macc. 12:39–13:23). Simon, whom the people acclaimed as commander, ethnarch, and high priest (1 Macc. 14:25–49), was even murdered by his own power-seeking son-in-law (16:11–24). Many in Israel regarded the Maccabean high priests as interlopers, and some of the pious left the city forever under the leadership of a priest in whose teaching they perceived divine inspiration and formed a community at the Dead Sea. They rejected the sacrificial cult of the Temple because it was carried out by wicked priests. Because of the many battles and conflicts the Romans finally came into the land and set themselves up as governing authorities in Jerusalem. Violent zeal for the Torah had led to new servitude.

Jesus walked through the city in order to make it and its mysterious history spiritually his own (Josh. 1:11). Seeing various kinds of activity which called anew for the severe words of the prophets, his feet were striding over that place where the eyes of the Lord remained and where he had placed his name for all time (1 Kings 9:3).

The Fascination of the Temple
and the Den of Thieves

Jesus'. disciples had often been in the Temple, but every time they were in wonder again over the size and splendor of the place. The mighty Temple court, the forecourt of the gentiles, was enclosed on all four sides by long porticos in which a busy coming and going of people prevailed. Groups of pilgrims stood or sat together to sing the holy songs of Israel. Scribes had gathered their students about them, and numerous merchants busied themselves with their wares and sacrificial animals. Jesus passed all of them silently and came to the northern portico, where a steep stairway led up to Fort Antonia, in which Roman soldiers had their quarters. Was this fort, which loomed high over the place of the Temple, not a sign of how the entire sacred area was in the hands of the pagans?

From the great court one reached an elevated area by steps to the inner court of the Temple, which was bordered on all sides by a lower wall — the wall of separation between Jew and gentile. In the middle of this inner court the main sanctuary of the Temple rose up; its huge facade looked toward the rising sun and was extended into the courtyards. Entering from the east, Jesus went through the Beautiful Gate into the Women's Court and from there he climbed with his disciples — as the women stood back — to the Court of Israel. Since they were laymen they were not allowed to go farther. But they saw further to where the priests were, where the altar of burnt offerings stood and behind which the facade of the house of the Temple rose. The tall and wide gate stood open. But a curtain veiled the inner recess of the sanctuary from the view of the laity, and only the high priest could enter the Holy of Holies with the blood of atonement one time each year. A fascination, which made all react in fright and shuddering, proceeded from this place.

Jesus stopped there for some time as he gazed steadily at the great curtain. Contradictory thoughts struggled within him. With his inner eye he saw how the glory of the Lord illuminated the earth and came from the east into the Temple like the sound of many waters (Ezek. 43:2–3) in order to make his name dwell there for all peoples (Isa. 18:7). At the same time he heard within himself the prophetic words against this place and the deceptive cries of the crowd: **The temple of the Lord, this is the temple of the Lord** (Jer. 7:4). The blood of animals carried by the high priest into the Holy of Holies — how could it reconcile Israel with God when the hearts of the people were so hard and closed, as he had experienced in his own preaching? How could the high priest, who was regarded even as the evil priest by the Dead Sea community, be so cleansed of his sins by the blood of a young bull (Lev. 16:6) so that he would be pleasing to God in representing Israel? While the questions and images whirled around in his soul the time for the evening offering by fire had come (Num. 28:3, 8). When a priest lifted the knife to the lamb that was led innocently to the altar, he remembered many words which had often struck him like sharp arrows, and he immediately envisioned himself as a lamb that would soon be slain.

After a long silence he turned around abruptly, left the Temple, and returned with his disciples to Bethany. The odor of burnt flesh followed him. His heart and mind were clear concerning the city, but the Temple, with its sacred luster, remained an open question and wound for him. He felt most profoundly that the Temple with its dividing walls and sacrificial rites opposed him, and likewise the hearts attached to these walls, sacrifices, and traditions.

Into the night songs could be heard which were sung in a slow, sustained fashion.

> **Come now, praise the Lord,**
> **all you servants of the Lord,**
> **who stand by night in the Lord's house.**
> (Ps. 134:1)

When the disciples and pilgrims had already long covered themselves with their mantles and lain down to sleep, the words of praise in the house of the Lord continued to ring in Jesus. They were connected to prophetic oracles about the nations, who would make pilgrimage to Jerusalem from all ends of the earth in order to praise the Lord on Zion.

On the next day he went back with the disciples to the Temple, led by the inner voice. When the loud shouting of the money-changers and the yells of the merchants came like waves against him, a deep indignation and a feeling of anger welled up in him (1 Sam. 11:6). All of a sudden it became clear to him what sign he must perform to claim the Temple for his Abba. He went to a group of money-changers and turned their tables over, so that the money rolled off onto the ground. Then he tore open the cages of some sellers of doves and let them fly away. He drove away sheep which were offered for sale. The merchants and money-changers, so suddenly disrupted in their businesses, drew back in confusion, and the scribes and Pharisees, who were nearby, were scared to the bone because they feared an uprising in the holy precincts. Some ran to report the disturbance to the Temple police, others managed to form a group and went to the disrupter of the sacred order of things. Jesus shouted to the startled crowd,

Have you not heard what the Scripture says?

My house will be called a house of prayer for all nations.
(Isa. 56:7)

Israel and foreigners from all nations and the most distant lands shall thank the Lord in it and give praise to him (2 Chron. 6:32). *But what have you made of it? A den of thieves!* (Jer. 7:11).

The scribes weren't impressed with his accusation, and one of them shot back to him: "In the same Scripture passage it says that the converted gentiles will present burnt offerings and sacrifice and will find favor with the Lord" (Isa. 56:7). How can you reject what is pleasing to God?" Jesus countered him sharply:

Read in the prophet Malachi which sacrifices please the Lord! Not disgusting foods, but pure offerings, which from the rising of the sun to its setting are brought to the Lord everywhere on the earth (Mal. 1:11). *Also the prophet Hosea says the same:*

For I desire steadfast love and not sacrifice,
knowledge of God, rather than burnt offerings.
(Hos. 6:6)

Because you don't obey the Lord, you will therefore become a laughing stock and a byword among the peoples (2 Chron. 7:19–20).

The scribes were provoked and irritated, and they shouted, "How can you dare to revile the Temple?" As the dispute grew, Jesus felt that his Father dwelled in him as in a temple and a deeper peace came over him. With a calm which disconcerted his opponents he spoke into the uproar, *Tear this temple down and I will erect another one in a few days.* Some screamed, "He blasphemes." Others laughed mockingly: "He speaks like a madman. It took our fathers forty-six years to build this Temple. How will he rebuild it in a few days?" (They deliberately left out that Herod had had the Temple built.)

Meanwhile the Temple security guards hurried up to them, followed by a group of priests. Since they saw Jesus in dispute with scribes and the merchants and money-changers had put their tables back up, they didn't immediately grasp what had happened. Most of the pilgrims on the broad Temple area seemed hardly to have noticed the action in the portico, and an arrest would only provoke a new and even greater uproar. The Pharisees and the Sadducaic priests, who always otherwise were at odds with each other, angrily discussed the incident and found themselves unanimously united against Jesus. Now they believed they had clear evidence that this false prophet from Galilee not only scorned the Torah but openly attacked the sacrificial liturgy in the Temple. This aroused especially the Sadducaic priests who served in the Temple and made their living by it. They all agreed that they should proceed with the sharpness of the Torah against the disrupter of the sacred order.

The opponents moved farther away, while the Temple security remained back to observe what would occur. Jesus heard the whispering of his enemies and saw how the priests and scribes withdrew in an obvious unanimity. He knew that the final decision had been made. The enemy ranks were approaching him in darkness in order to seize him.

Waiting for the Hour

In Bethany Jesus and the twelve were invited for a meal by Simon the Leper. While they reclined at the table they talked about the time of the exile, when Israel had no Temple after the Babylonian army had destroyed the holy city. Then the conversation turned to the great Day of Atonement. Jesus himself said little, leading the discussion rather through questions to his meal companions. What seemed to interest him above all was the meaning they attributed to that atonement ritual in which the high priest transferred the sins of all Israel onto the head of a goat, who was then driven out into the wilderness. But no one had ever really thought about it, and they knew only that it had been so written in the Torah.

During the meal a woman with a jar of alabaster came. She broke the glass at the small neck and let a part of the oil streaming out flow onto the head of Jesus. With the remainder she anointed his feet. The aroma of the costly ointment filled the entire space. The guests were taken by surprise. Some saw it as an extravagance and showed their displeasure openly. Judas said calmly and coldly, "The oil could have sold for more than three hundred denarii and we could have given the money to the poor." Several agreed with him. Jesus, however, turned his full attention to the woman, who crouched confused and embarrassed at his feet. He said to them, while gazing at her:

Why do you understand her not and trouble her? Don't you remember?

As long as the king lies on the couch
my nard gives forth its fragrance.
(Song 1:12)

Likewise this woman's nard will give forth its fragrance as long as people speak of God's kingdom. You will always have the poor among you, and you can act as their neighbors at any time. But this woman has done here and now what she was able to do. Yes, her open heart has prompted her to a prophetic sign. In her love she has anointed my body in advance for burial.

These last words had the effect of a shock on the host and guests and caused them to forget everything else. Why did Jesus speak of his burial? They were bewildered, but they couldn't bring themselves to ask further questions. But the woman, who had overheard the words about burial, seemed in her open helplessness to emit a fragrance like a nard.

They ended the meal in a depressed mood. Then Jesus drew the twelve and the other followers close to him and tried to give them hope. *Don't be afraid of those who can kill the body, but be glad that you are written in the book of life. The Lord will rescue you all from death.*

They had been thinking only about the coming kingdom and had given scarcely a thought to death. Aroused by the new tone in his discourse, one in the circle timidly asked him, "Why does it say in one of Israel's hymns, **The dead do not praise the Lord** (Ps. 115:17)?" Since they were all familiar with the doctrine of the Sadducees, that there was no resurrection of the dead, they pricked up their ears. What would Jesus' answer be? He spoke:

> *Only those can no longer praise the Lord who are possessed by sin; they are already dead on earth because they are removed from the source of life. But the God of Abraham, Isaac, and Jacob* (Exod. 3:6) *does not let those who have died sink down into the dust of the forgotten. He is a God of the living and not of the dark kingdom of death. The underworld lies open before him.* (Prov. 15:11)

But the hearts of the disciples were still disturbed, and one of them asked further: "The Pharisees believe in a resurrection of the dead, but they teach that all who die early or are killed are given over to this terrible fate as punishment for their sins. Can those who are judged by God himself still praise him in the realm of death? Are they not forever shadows under his wrath?" Jesus was silent for some time, and then spoke as tension grew: *Job was right to defend himself against his friends, who were really his enemies. In his misfortune they wanted to convince him of his guilt, yet they didn't know the mysterious ways of the Lord.* "What are the mysterious ways? Can you explain them to us?" the disciples asked. With lips which spread deep knowledge (Prov. 15:7), Jesus answered:

> *The prophet Isaiah saw in visions the Servant of the Lord. He is anointed by the Spirit of the Lord and struck down and murdered because of the people's sins. But God did not reject him. Because he offered his life as an atonement-offering for others, the Lord was pleased with him and delivered him from the snares of death in order to give him a portion in his kingdom.* (Isa. 53)

These words continued to reverberate in the silence that followed. The disciples intuited more than they understood. How could some slain or executed person find favor with God? Why was he an atonement-offering? Thomas tried to fathom what remained obscure to him, asking, "How can the Servant of God give over his life as an atonement-offering? Wouldn't he then let himself be slaughtered like a lamb on the altar? Aren't human sacrifices an abomination to God, deeds of murder which arouse his anger?" Jesus replied immediately, *Yes, the Lord is deeply offended when people spill the blood of their brothers and sisters.* After a long pause he added,

> *Can you grasp that the Son of Man acts as a neighbor even to those who have murderous hearts? Innocent as a lamb he goes after the lost and seeks after them without regarding what might happen to him and what they do to him.*

John asked, agitated and uncertain, "Will God not protect the Messiah in every way and destroy his enemies? Jesus said to him in words full of warmth and trust,

> *Yes, God will protect him and never let him slip out of his hand. But do you understand the word of the Lord through the prophet Jeremiah?*

> **I have given the beloved of my soul**
> **into the hands of her enemies.**
>   (Jer. 12:7)

A depressed silence followed these words, while the song of a group of pilgrims could be heard in the distance.

> **Be gracious to me, O Lord, for I am in distress;**
> **for grief my eye, my soul, my body are wasted.** . . . .
> **I hear the whispering of the multitude — terror on every side!**
> **They scheme together against me,**
> **they plot to take my life.** (Ps. 31:9, 13)

For the disciples it was as if they themselves had heard a whispering, and a terror began to surround them on every side.

The Final Controversy

When Jesus went back into the city and into the Temple, he knew he was in danger. He entrusted each of his steps to the Father, went innocently as a lamb (Jer. 11:19), and yet watched with the cleverness of a serpent for possible signs to point his way. When Pharisees and scribes noticed his return, some of them went up to him and tried to test him again. "By what authority do you teach the people and interpret the Scripture? You have not attended any school." Jesus perceived the ambush they had conceived, and he let them rush into the net that they had stretched to trap him (Ps. 9:15): *But tell me first by what authority John preached! Was he a prophet? Did his baptism come from God or only from himself?* The question created confusion, and the scribes knew immediately that they themselves had fallen into the role of being tested. They conferred among themselves in low voices. What kind of rejoinder could they make? If they acknowledged John's authority as coming from God, they would have to deal with further painful questions from Jesus. If they answered to the contrary, that his baptism was only a human work, then they feared the reactions among the many pilgrims who listened to their dispute. Many of the people had believed in the Baptizer, and since his execution he had won even more esteem. They decided thus to avoid an answer and said, "We don't know." Jesus took up their answer:

> *If you don't know with what authority John baptized, how will you then understand the authority that was given to me by the Father? But since you are all well schooled you can certainly answer another question for me: Whose son will the Messiah be when he comes?*

They were happy to leave the theme that had become embarrassing for them, and they answered, "David's." He questioned them further:

*Why did the great King say when he prophetically envisioned the
Messiah,*

> The Lord says to my lord:
> Sit at my right hand,
> till I make your enemies your footstool.
>
> (Ps. 110:1)

How could David address the Messiah as lord if this one is his son?

The scribes stood there speechless. Although they had often spoken
among themselves about the awaited Messiah and knew quite well the
psalm that Jesus cited, the question in this sense had never occurred
to them nor had it been asked. Again they began to take counsel with
one another. One said he heard from his teacher that the Messiah
had been hidden by God since the beginning of creation and would
come at the end of days to redeem Israel. Perhaps he was actually
not David's son and the great king himself wanted to intimate this
in a psalm. Others, however, immediately objected that the Scripture
witnessed quite clearly that an everlasting promise belonged to the
House of David (2 Sam. 7:12–16), and it taught unambiguously that
the Messiah would grow as a shoot out of the tree stump of Jesse (Isa.
11:1) and would come forth from Bethlehem (Mic. 5:1).

> Of his sovereignty
> and of peace there will be no end,
> upon the throne of David, and over his kingdom,
> to establish and support it with righteousness
> now and forever more. (Isa. 9:7)

So the scribes had no answer and were perplexed. That he was able to
ask such questions meant he had another way of reading the Scripture
with which they were unfamiliar and which disturbed them. There
was only one thing to do: the dangerous spirit that spoke from him
must be reduced to silence.

Jesus read their thoughts and this constrained him to bring darkness out of light (Dan. 2:22). So he began to recount a parable to the people listening.

> *A man planted a vineyard on a fertile hill; he dug a pit for a wine press and built a tower in the middle of it* (Isa. 5:1–2). *He let it out to vinedressers so that they would work it and he could obtain its fruit. At the time of harvest he sent a servant to get his portion of the fruits. The tenants, however, took him and beat him. Then he sent a second servant, whom the tenants almost killed. The owner said to himself, "Perhaps they didn't recognize my servants." And he sent a third. But they even killed him. Now the owner said, "They will certainly show respect to my own son." But when the tenants saw the son coming they banded together: "Come on! This is the heir; let's kill him and the land is ours." They slew him and cast him out of the vineyard.*

When the listeners began to get worked up about the evil vinedressers, Jesus asked them, *What will the owner do with the murderers?* From every side they shouted to him, "He will repay evil with evil and slay the murderers!" Jesus responded, *So human beings think and act. But the Lord will bring to pass a miracle before the eyes of his people.*

The stone that the builders rejected
has become the cornerstone.

(Ps. 118:22)

The people didn't understand this response; only the scribes presumed that Jesus had meant them with the murderous vinedressers. They became indignant about it and in their anger they had already forgotten what they had just said among themselves. They were also disturbed because they correctly assumed Jesus meant himself with the son in the parable. "Does he exalt himself over all others in Israel? Will he alone be the chosen Son of God?" They angrily turned their backs on him.

Jesus noticed that Judas had withdrawn from the twelve. Events were coming to a head and taking their course. Therefore he wanted to make provision for the imminent Passover meal, that he could at least observe it without being interrupted by the evil forces. He dismissed his disciples and went alone to a house where, on pilgrimages in prior years, he had often eaten the Passover lamb with his relatives from Nazareth. He made an appointment for two of his disciples to meet with the servant of the landlord. Then he left the city. He was caught up in thought: with what signs would he take his departure from his disciples?

The Bride to Be Cleansed

Toward evening a group of pilgrims from Galilee arrived in Bethany. Among them was Mary. Jesus had not seen his mother for a long time and he was surprised at how she had changed. She radiated a strange beauty and a mature calmness which could have emerged only out of many inward pains. All motherly features had fallen away from her, and she met Jesus like a woman who had accompanied him on his way from a distance, but with great love and profound participation. He embraced her tenderly, and she delivered to him a new robe (1 Sam. 2:19) whose undergarment was woven without a seam from top to bottom. He took it gratefully, seeing it as a sign of coming events (Ps. 22:18). He didn't need to tell her much about what he had done meanwhile in public. She had had it all reported to her, preserving and bearing it in her heart. Also for her part she had only to indicate the reactions of relatives and acquaintances, who caused her so much suffering (Job 19:13–14). He understood, as he had long felt it all within. She posed no questions about what he planned or expected; he gave her only to understand that he awaited everything hour by hour from the Father. She understood this without grasping the details. Silently, and deeply present to one another, they remained sitting beside each other for a long while. When Mary returned to the pilgrims with whom she had come, she went away from him like a woman who bore a great burden, but who precisely through it had found a mysterious peace and maturity.

Jesus lingered yet for some time at the spot where his meeting with Mary had occurred. His memory wandered back into the years in Nazareth, and his entire past life passed by again in images. The coming of his mother had spoken to the deep spaces of the past in him and made them live once more. At the same time he perceived therein the announcement of a final departure. He let both vibrate together within him. Regarding the expected departure, the determination of the last great sign grew out of the images of the past.

While he reflected on the images and forces that moved him, voices in the vicinity began to sing softly. At first he didn't listen, but suddenly his attention was caught by the words sounding toward him:

> Beautiful are you, my love,
> behold, you are beautiful!
> Your eyes are like doves
> behind your veil.
> Your hair like a flock of goats
> moving down the slopes of Gilead.
> Your lips like scarlet threads,
> lovely is your mouth.
> Your breasts are like twins of a gazelle
> feeding in the lilies.
> When the day breathes away and the shadows grow
> I will go to the mountain of myrrh,
> to the hill of frankincense.
> Everything in you is lovely, my love,
> in you there is no flaw. (Song 4:1, 3, 5–7)

The words sung floated through the trees of the garden, and it was difficult to know where they came from. For Jesus they became woven into a picture which for a moment made him remember his mother again. This was replaced by another image: Yahweh chose his people as his bride and married her:

> And when I passed by you and saw you lying in your blood, I
> said to you in your blood, "Live, and grow up like a plant of
> the field." And you grew tall and blossomed gloriously. Your
> breasts were formed, your hair was thick. Yet you were naked
> and bare. Then I passed by you and saw you, and behold, you
> were at the age for love. I spread my skirt over you and covered
> your nakedness. Yea, I plighted my troth to you and entered
> into a covenant with you, and you were mine. (Ezek. 16:6–8)

The blossoming young woman quickly became a prostitute. God promised her everlasting faithfulness, yet the chosen one immediately became involved with rivals. Jesus suddenly felt, with great intensity, the tenderness of his Abba while his spirit moved from the prophetic image to the people he had encountered in recent months. Weren't they like a faded prostitute? They went through their days tired and dull like a prisoner. In their desires they were thrown back on themselves, in small and dreary greed, and what they believed to profit them was really like a net in which they snared themselves. Jesus saw leprosy on their bodies and deadly wounds in their hearts, wounds so deep that the afflicted scarcely noticed anything wrong. Resignation was written on them, but they themselves held it as wisdom and cleverness. He could not find in them the beautiful beloved in the song, the daughter of the king who comes to him (Ps. 45:10), nor could he perceive the bride with whom he desired to appear before his Abba. He must first cleanse and heal her by his own self-giving. Her love had quickly become extinguished in her youth, but through his love he wanted to make her love blossom anew (Isa. 54:6).

His disciples appeared in his reflections. A good will, like the aroma of a spring blossom, lived in them. But at the same time they would have to bear a heavy burden which would make their steps difficult and their eyes dim. They heard his words, but they didn't yet resound in their hearts. When would the reign of his Father fully break in? He thought about the feast with the finest foods that God will prepare for all nations on Mt. Zion (Isa. 25:6). Suddenly the sign struck him with which he wanted to take leave from his disciples: he had to become one with them, like husband and wife when they become one flesh. He would give himself to them at the meal.

The Farewell Sign of Love and the Betrayal

The disciples asked him where the Passover meal should be made ready. Also Judas inquired. Jesus gave Simon and John the task of going into the city and informed them where a man with a large water jar would be waiting for them. They should follow him, and in the house where he would lead them they would prepare the meal. The pair did as they were instructed. They bought a lamb without blemish, as well as unleavened bread, wine, bitter herbs, and purée (Exod. 12:1–11). At noon they went up to the Temple to slaughter the lamb with the rest of the mass of people who were doing the same. Priests took up the blood and poured it at the foot of the altar.

After sundown Jesus showed up, with the rest of the disciples from the circle of the twelve, where Simon and John had prepared the meal. Following the ritual prescription they solemnly reclined — as a sign of freedom after the exodus out of Egypt, the house of slavery — at the table. Shortly after the initial blessing Jesus suddenly stopped. With a sadness out of keeping with the joy of the feast he said, *One of my friends will soon betray me* (Ps. 31:13). The words fell like a lightning flash onto the circle. Some exclaimed almost simultaneously, "Surely it's not me, Master!" while others could hardly believe that one of them could be so unfaithful and presumptuous. Jesus made it still clearer:

> *It is one whom I have chosen myself and who now eats with me* (Ps. 41:9), *who dips his hand in the bowl. The Son of Man goes his way, as it is written in the Scripture. But woe to that man by whom the Son is handed over to sinners. He will fall into the harshest judgment.*

Immediately then Jesus began to eat some of the bitter herbs, which now no longer recalled only the bitter wilderness, but also invoked the bitterness of this hour. When the disciples made the circle tighter around him and Judas dipped his hand in the bowl, Jesus dipped his hand too. Judas looked at him in distress and asked in a quiet, anguished voice, "Do you mean me?" Jesus replied only, *You know what you are doing.*

After giving praise to God and thanks for the liberation from Egypt, Jesus reminded the twelve of the manna that was given to the people in the wilderness. Then he began to speak about a new food from heaven which the Father would soon provide. He took the bread, broke it into pieces, and handed it to the disciples with the words, *Take and eat, this is my body.* The disciples were confused, for they realized, without understanding the import of the words, that the ritual of the meal had been broken. They took the bread offered, ate it, and began right away to eat the lamb. With the concluding cup of blessing Jesus said a long prayer. He praised the Father for the works of creation and thanked him for the gracious gift of the covenant (Exod. 24:5–8). He spoke of the slave-house of sin in which Israel and the nations were still held prisoner, and of a new covenant (Jer. 31:31–34) which is no longer concluded with the blood of animals like the covenant at Sinai. Then he gave the cup to his disciples with the words, *This is my blood, the blood of the covenant, which is poured out for many.* The disciples were attentive but perplexed. Had not Moses strictly prohibited the eating of blood (Lev. 17:10–14)? What did this strange sign have to do with the blood of their master? Jesus said insistently, *What the Torah rejected the Father turns into the source of true life. The Son of Man gives the blood that is shed by evil-doers as blood of the covenant that binds everyone to him.* The disciples assented, with hesitation, and they drank. Then he continued:

> *With longing I have awaited this meal of departure with you. After I leave you, do what I have done for you in memory of me. I will not drink again of the fruit of the vine until I drink it anew with you in the kingdom of my Father.*

For the disciples his words continued to be dark and hidden. But since an oppressive burden already lay on them and they had become used to not understanding much of what he said, they did not question him further.

Their meal ended in spite of great sadness with the joyful Hallel, the common song of praise (Pss. 115–18), and they thanked God for his everlasting grace. Then they set out. Through dark side streets in which numerous pilgrims were still making their way they left the city and went to the Kidron Valley. On the way Jesus said, *I have prayed to God that he deliver you from the enemies who will soon come. When the shepherd is struck down the flock disintegrates and the sheep are scattered* (Zech. 13:7). *But I will soon gather you anew.* Peter interrupted him: "We will stand beside you whatever may come." The others made similar vows. Jesus replied only, *Already in the morning when the rooster crows, it will be otherwise than you say.*

According to the Torah pilgrims must spend Passover night in Jerusalem, so they did not return to Bethany. On the eastern slope of the Kidron Valley, which was part of the city, Jesus entered a country estate with olive trees where there was an old winepress. In earlier years, when he traveled to Jerusalem with Galilean pilgrims, he had usually spent Passover night here. In this olive orchard he now let his disciples camp. He noticed that Judas was missing. This disciple, whom he had identified with the gesture at the meal, had remained a little behind in the dark, and as soon as he saw that the others went onto the estate, he turned quickly back to the city.

Jesus took with him those three disciples who had accompanied him to the mountain beyond the Jordan. He walked only a stone's throw away and asked them to persist in prayer with him. Immediately then his whole body began to shake. The great confidence with which he had gone on his way in spite of the threat of danger and the blessed joy that had constantly flowed to him from his Father — they vanished all at once. Something broke apart in his soul and an abyss to sorrow and confusion opened its jaws (Ps. 22:13). He fell into a deep pit and floods of despair billowed over his head (Ps. 69:15), while the Father concealed his countenance from him (Ps. 30:7). His bones were torn from their joints and his heart melted like wax (Ps. 22:14). Staggering (Isa. 24:20), he moved away from his disciples, threw himself on the ground, and began groaning and crying out, *Father, everything is possible for you. Let this cup of staggering pass from me!* Then he added with all the effort of his will, *Yet not what I will, but what you will be done.* He remained for a long time in this struggle until his desire to find comfort from his disciples was overwhelming; but in the meanwhile they had fallen asleep from sadness and fatigue, although they had perceived his shaking and crying. He called them to wake up and complained in his misery, *Couldn't you stay awake with me one hour? Watch and pray, so that you won't fall into the pit of despair!* As soon as he drew away from them again he fell once more to the ground. He wrestled with the night in him, while sweat ran out of his pores. With his will he held to the faithfulness of the Father, but there was raging in his body and soul against it (Jer. 4:19), and he didn't succeed in overcoming the storm of this revolt. When he returned to his disciples after some time, he again found no help from them, for their eyes were closed and spent with grief (Lam. 2:11). So he continued anew the lonely struggle. When the uproar within him abated somewhat, he saw in the darkness many torches quickly coming closer. He awoke his disciples: *Get up, for the hour has come when the judgment of sin begins.*

Thrown into the Abyss of Death

The torches were carried by the servants of the high priest, who also brought clubs and swords with them. Judas was with them. He stepped quickly up to Jesus, said hurriedly "Rabbi," and kissed him. Immediately the circle closed around them (Ps. 86:14). While some of the disciples tried to defend themselves, someone among the band that came after Jesus took out his sword, but in the confusion he struck only a servant of the high priest. Jesus spoke loudly to his disciples and the band from the high priest: *All who live by the sword shall die by the sword.* Meanwhile he didn't try to defend himself and was captured. When his disciples saw that he was taken they fled — each for himself alone (1 Sam. 4:10), and the darkness closed over them (Mic. 3:6). Only Simon remained behind, protected by the darkness.

The arresters, while it was still night, led Jesus to the house of the high priest Caiaphas, where in the meantime many members of the high council had been hastily summoned and were waiting. When Jesus was led before the priests, elders, and scribes, whispering and murmuring passed through those gathered (Ps. 31:13). The rivalries and differences of opinion that usually prevailed among them seemed now to be swept away, and they were happy about this. Their roles as council authorities and their awareness of serving the Temple and the Torah pushed aside all personal questions and doubts. As they, the many, looked with secret triumph at the one, who stood lonely and alone before them (Ps. 25:2, 16), they felt themselves to be of one mind (Ps. 41:7).

Simon had followed in the darkness as Jesus was led away by the band. When they disappeared through the gate at the house of the high priest, he ventured, after some hesitation, to step out into the forecourt. He thought that probably no one would know him among the people who had gathered there. Suddenly, however, a maid stepped up to him in the light of the fire burning in the court and said to the bystanders, "I saw this one with him just a little while ago." Simon shrank back and began to shake. Hastily and without thinking he denied it: "No, I don't know him." But now many of the bystanders had taken notice of him. The maid repeated her re-mark and Simon denied it even more vehemently. But by now the bystanders were saying loudly, "He was certainly with him, because he's a Galilean. We can tell by his speech." Fear ran through Simon body and soul, and he started invoking wild curses on himself. He cried out and swore, "I'll be damned if I know the man you're talk-ing about at all!" Some said, "Leave him in peace! The main thing is that he wants nothing to do with the man taken inside." One fellow even pounded him good-naturedly on the shoulder and said, "Don't get upset! The high authorities know what they have to do. We don't want to get mixed up in their affairs." Simon drew back hurriedly from the glow of the fire and left the forecourt in the protection of the nameless crowd.

Meanwhile inside the house a hearing had begun in which the entire weight of a long tradition was marshalled to attack Jesus. Scribes from the party of the Pharisees came forward: "We have heard from Galilee that you despise the Torah. Confess that you're guilty!" Yet on the further question as to where and when he spoke or acted against the Torah no witnesses who agreed with each other could be found (Deut. 17:6). Then the Sadducees gave their opinion and had new witnesses appear (Job 10:17): "You ridiculed the Temple liturgy and said you would tear down the Temple and rebuild it in three days." But also here the witnesses did not agree. The collapse of the accusation only heightened the tension, for from the prisoner there radiated such a calmness, indeed a majesty, that already his appearance both irritated and attracted them (Wisd. 2:15). The anxiety of each one infected the other, so that *all* the council authorities were carried away by *one* thing: to condemn and expel that one who challenged them with his strange authority.

The high priest intervened in the tense situation and demanded sternly with the solemn voice of his office, "Do you not respond to the accusations that are raised against you?" Since Jesus remained silent, the high council had no further plan for the hearing. Without really knowing what he was doing the high priest stepped into the middle and adjured the accused by the living God: "Tell us, are you the Messiah, the Son of the Blessed?" Jesus looked around the circle of his accusers and did what they had not dared hope of him. He affirmed publicly and did not deny it: *Yes, I am the one. That one you scorn as a worm and the son of man* (Job 25:6) *God will elevate to his right hand* (Ps. 110:1) *and make him become the Son of Man on the clouds of heaven* (Dan. 7:13). Then all the council members sprang up, held their ears, and cried from all sides, "Blasphemy! Blasphemy against God!" The high priest, reacting quickly with a ritual gesture, tore a small piece of his robe at the neck and cried out to the agitated gathering, "What do we still need with witnesses? You have heard the blasphemy. What is your judgment?" As if from a dark background the response resounded unanimously, "He is deserving of death!"

Jesus felt as if a mysterious mark was burned into his forehead and body, and he spoke out with the voice of a prophet: *The net with which you catch me will trap you* (Job 18:7–10), *and the word of judgment will be changed to viper's venom in your mouth* (Job 20:12–14). Rash servants who wanted to please the high priest and the council members made faces at him, struck his cheeks with insolence, and ganged up against him (Job 16:10). They made him the butt of their mockery and spit in his face (Job 17:6). His clean body was pasted with filth. The chief priest, elders, and scribes became more and more aroused: "He despises the Torah that God himself established (Deut. 17:12). What presumption to assert that God will raise him up and install him as judge over us! He will soon know that the Lord casts to the ground the wickedness of the one who stretches out his hand against the Almighty" (Job 15:25). The high priest stretched out his hand and shouted as if out of his mind or in prophetic frenzy (1 Sam. 10:10): "May all the guilt that you have revived in Israel be placed on your head" (Lev. 16:21).

In the early morning they led Jesus bound to Fort Antonia in order to hand him over to the Roman governor. The council authorities had agreed among themselves to accuse him before Pilate of rebellion against the occupying power. For hadn't he himself said he was the Messiah? He must therefore be planning a revolt, for the king of Israel anointed by God (Ps. 72) could not begin his reign under foreign sovereignty. Hadn't the Galilean pilgrims already acclaimed him as king when they entered the city with messianic shouts some days ago? They were only hoping that he would admit his messianic pretensions just as openly to the Roman governor as he had before them. If he did that, no further argument would be needed.

The members of the council remained standing in the northern portico of the Temple before the long stairway that led up to the fortress and requested that the Roman governor come to them. As soon as Pilate appeared, surrounded by soldiers, they began to accuse Jesus. The governor had him led back into the fortress and began his own hearing. "Are you the Messiah, the king of the Jews?" Jesus replied, "Do you ask me this question of your own volition, or do you do it only because others accuse me?" Pilate rejoined, "The matters of your faith don't trouble me, but the leaders of your people have given you over to me. What have you done?" Jesus was silent and offered no defense. This was very much a surprise to the governor. So he went again to the council authorities to gain more precise information concerning why they had delivered to him this strange man for punishment. The chief priest and elders accused him of being no friend of the Romans (1 Macc. 8), for in Galilee he had begun to proclaim a new sovereign rulership and he had come to Jerusalem with this objective.

When Pilate heard that Jesus came from Galilee, the district of Herod, he sent him to the tetrarch, who was currently passing some time in Jerusalem. Jesus, however, said nothing in response to his wordy speech (Job 11:1). All the more vehemently the council leaders accused him. He wanted to set himself up as king and endangered all law and order. However, Herod and his officers had heard nothing dangerous about him in Galilee. Nevertheless, since their curiosity about seeing a miracle was disappointed, they turned the accusation into a farce. They had Jesus dressed in the dirty remains of royal attire for official occasions and sent him back to Pilate like that. This game pleased the Roman governor, as he immediately comprehended how the ruler of Galilee evaluated the accusations against this royal pretender. Above all it pleased him that the Jewish ruler knew how to create a scene of mockery out of the fanatical attacks of the council authorities. So from then on both dictators, these smoking stumps of firebrands (Isa. 7:4), became friends, although before they had long been enemies.

Meanwhile, in the portico in front of the fortress a large group from the people had assembled; they wanted to ask for the release of someone owing to the customary Passover amnesty. Shortly before there had been a disturbance in which someone had been killed. The result was that the rioters — and with them a certain Barabbas — were arrested by the Roman soldiers. When Pilate came out of the fortress again after Jesus had been led away, petitioners immediately stepped forward to intercede for Barabbas. Now the governor wanted to continue the mocking game (Jer. 20:7) begun by Herod and the same time to settle this whole Jesus business. So he offered to release for them the king in his shabby royal garments. But the council members were zealously at work in the assembled throng, which slowly grew larger, and provoked them all to demand the freeing of Barabbas. The people became caught up in senselessness, like a dove (Hos. 7:11). First one shouted, then all the others, "Barabbas, Barabbas should go free!"

The governor saw that his cruel game was going amiss. In the pose of a serious judge who had already lost his case he asked, "What should be done with this king?" The answer was a resounding shout: "Crucify him! Crucify him!" Gentiles who were located in the outer forecourt and who followed the events out of curiosity were swept up in the contagion of the yelling mob and joined their voices in the cry to crucify him. Pilate asked theatrically what crime the king had committed that was worthy of death. Some council authorities cried, "We have a Torah, and according to it he must die because he elevated himself to the right hand of God. Satan, who tries to take the place of God, speaks through him." Although Pilate did not understand what they meant by this accusation, it came across to him as uncanny and weird. Therefore he wanted nothing more to do with the case and to dispose of it as fast as possible.

He gave the command to scourge Jesus, and he turned him over for execution. The soldiers welcomed this outcome, for this would let them continue the game begun by Herod and break their monotonous daily routine. They led Jesus into the fortress, called the entire cohort together, pressed a crown of thorns on his head, and gave him a reed as a scepter in his hand. Then they laughed and danced around him, bowed before him, and hailed him as king of the Jews, while belching and spitting in his face. After that they grabbed the scourge, took off his garments, and repeatedly struck him in mirthful excitement.

The circle had closed around him. Bulls of Bashan were surrounding him, and ravening, roaring lions opened their mouths at him

(Ps. 22:12–16). As the mock king he experienced the way in which all those like Herod and Pilate, as figures representing rulers of the world, were in league against the Son (Ps. 2:2). When the soldiers gripped the scourge, they appeared to him in all his pain as like a violent horde, that of Gog and Magog (Ezek. 38:1–15), which was drawing near from all the ends of the earth. Evil struck his body with full weight; the accusation of blasphemy made him a curse for Israel and among the nations (Zech. 8:13). His soul trembled as trees shake in the wind (Isa. 7:2), and his heart was wrung within him (Lam. 1:20). He had seen Satan fall from heaven. Now he felt that the great accuser had been released into the nameless mob and the faceless peoples of the earth. Poisonous arrows shot by an invisible hand penetrated into him from all sides (Ps. 64:3–4).

When the soldiers put his garments back on him, his body was completely covered with wounds which began to fester (Ps. 38:3–5). They laid the beam for a cross on his shoulders, which he could hardly carry, and led him out of the fortress. In front of the procession that moved toward the place of execution a soldier carried a sign with the inscription "King of the Jews." They encountered many people, who stood staring, laughed among themselves, and mocked this king (2 Chron. 36:16). The crucifixion beam lay like an infinitely heavy burden upon him (Ps. 38:4), and suddenly there rose up in his memory the image of that animal which, loaded with the sins of the entire people, was driven out of the city on the great Day of Atonement over almost the same route on which he was now being led. This recollection made the burden even heavier and he fell to the ground under it. The soldiers wrenched him back up, but they took the beam off him and compelled a man whom they picked up by chance from the people along the way to carry the timber to the place of execution.

In the throng by which he was led there were pilgrims from Galilee who had acclaimed him just a few days before. Some apprehensively kept back, while others quickly accommodated themselves to the new situation and said that the preacher from Nazareth had always been a suspicious character. None of the men dared give him a sign of friendship. Only among the women — whose status counted for little in public so they could give expression to their feelings without danger — were there some who pushed their way to him and, crying and lamenting, showed him their pain and sympathy. Jesus thanked them, but he said, *You daughters of Israel, don't wail over me. Wail above all for yourselves and your children. When this fate comes to me, what will happen to the city and the people?* He managed in his pain to say further,

> *To the barren who were once distressed and despised* (1 Sam. 1:1–16) *it will be said: "Happy the wombs that haven't given birth and the breasts that haven't given suck"; and to the mountains and hills that would bring blessing for Israel* (Ps. 72:3) *they will cry: "Fall on us and cover us!"* (Hos. 10:8). *Now it is already being revealed what will happen everywhere.*

At the site of execution, which was called Golgotha, the Place of the Skull, and where the traces of the many dead could be felt, someone extended to Jesus some painkilling wine which was mixed with vinegar (Ps. 69:22). He tasted a little of it but didn't want to drink it. Then the soldiers took his garments, nailed his hands to the beam, and placed him high on one of the stakes already standing there. Also they lifted the sign with the words "King of the Jews" onto the stake. Likewise the soldiers dragged two outlaws to the place, hanging one on the right and the other on the left of Jesus. They were to make up the bitterly comical high court of the King of the Jews (1 Kings 10:4–10). They divided the clothes of those crucified among themselves. They cast lots, however, for the outer robe of Jesus (Ps. 22:18), which his mother had woven from top to bottom without a seam.

Some of the priests, elders, and scribes wanted to make certain that Jesus was actually executed, and thus they had followed the procession to the Place of the Skull. Seeing how he was now hanging on the cross, they felt relieved and began to ridicule him. They lifted up mockingly against him what he had affirmed before the high council: "You passed yourself off as the Messiah-King and asserted God would raise you to his right hand. Now you're really elevated, but not on the clouds. If you are the chosen Son of Heaven, then climb down from the cross and have yourself borne up to God's right hand (Wisd. 2:17–18)! Then we will believe." Also pilgrims from Galilee who were standing there felt themselves encouraged to scoff. "He trusted in his miracles. If he actually has any power he can help himself. We want to see whether his confidence is anything more than a spider's web" (Job 8:14). But suddenly darkness came over the land which nobody could explain, and it seemed uncanny to everyone. The mockery stopped.

Since Jesus had refused the painkilling drink, the acts and words of his enemies penetrated painfully into his consciousness. His perception of the soldiers, who executed their task as a daily duty and didn't seem to notice whom their blows struck, was that of figures led by foreign powers and manipulated by foreign hands. The moment he was raised high up on the stake a severe and endlessly working surge of pain bored through his entire consciousness (Isa. 53:5). The words that ridiculed the work of his Father in him reached his soul only as if they were coming through a veil. They were like arrows shot by nameless archers. But they struck him exactly where he had experienced the blessed and tender presence of his Abba. He prayed for his enemies, *Father, forgive them, for they don't know what they are doing.* The evil into which the nameless figures had twisted the goodness of his Father (Ps. 56:5) he wanted once more to turn into love. Then all of a sudden he saw his disciple Judas before him. He too was hanging on a tree, twisting and turning in need and despair. But was it not true that

the Lord will never cease in his mercy,
nor cause any of his works to perish
(Sir. 47:22)

Jesus enfolded him completely into his own extreme distress, and many who were in similar despair as they wrestled with death seemed to follow him. He enfolded the faithless and desperate heart of his disciple (Hos. 2:12–13) and betrothed him anew (Hos. 2:19).

With that the complete horror of being without God filled him. He sank into the depths, the bottomless depths (Ps. 88:3–7). The farther he fell, the slower were the movements, until everything stood still. Time had stopped. Only a kind of space was there, without direction or goal, a place of nameless dread and agonizing anxieties, a world of eternal hopelessness. Out of the depth of his spirit a shout and cry broke out: *Eloi, Eloi, lema sabachtani? My God, my God, why have you forsaken me?* And then he gave himself into the hands of the one from whom he experienced himself as abandoned (Job 16:6–18).

Those standing around shuddered at the cry of agony. One of the scribes, who was trying stubbornly to withstand the dread that slipped in out of the darkness, ventured a final bit of mockery. He twisted "Eloi" (Ps. 56:5) and said in ridicule, "Listen, listen, he calls for Elijah" [Elia/Eliyah]. Now we'll see at any moment whether the prophet comes to rescue him." Everything became so quiet that it was uncanny to the mocker. But Jesus let out again with a cry which penetrated to the marrow of everyone, even the stupefied solders, and which made heaven and earth shake (Joel 3:16). Then he sank back into himself and died.

Age-old graves in the area appeared to open in order to release forgotten and hushed up stories of injustice, deceit, and murder. At the same time a strange thing happened in the Temple. A tearing sound could be heard, and the curtain of the Holy of Holies was suddenly pulled off, without anyone knowing how this could have occurred. Priests, terrified, hurried there to try to put everything in order again. Laypeople, who got a quick glimpse of it, said the inner sanctuary was empty.

After Jesus' death cry one of the scribes standing there, hitherto silent, said: "Now we're sure he was a blasphemer because he was not delivered when he was at the edge of death (Ps. 30:3). God may let a righteous person enter into distress and the danger of death, but he doesn't abandon him to the underworld (Ps. 16:10), nor does he permit him to be condemned and killed (Ps. 37:33). **A man hanged is accursed by God**" (Deut. 21:23). The Roman centurion who commanded the soldiers at the crucifixion had followed the whole event observantly and silently. He responded to the last words of the scribe: "Are you absolutely sure he was a blasphemer? I've seen many men crucified, but none has ever died like this. Truly, he must be a son of God." The council officials shook their heads over this pagan and left.

At some distance women from Galilee, among whom were the mother of Jesus and Mary Magdalene, had followed the crucifixion and watched the death of Jesus in frustration and helplessness. When the priests and scribes returned to the city, they drew closer and saw that one of the soldiers was plunging his spear into the breast of the dead man. They looked at the one who was pierced and broke out in lament as for an only son (Zech. 12:10). Mary, the mother of Jesus, saw blood and water flow out of the side laid open and she remembered an oracle of the prophet Zechariah:

On that day a fountain will flow for the house of David and for the dwellers of Jerusalem to cleanse them from sin and uncleanness. (Zech. 13:1)

Mary Magdalene, on the other hand, spoke — as in a dream — of water which streamed from beneath the Temple (Ezek. 47:1).

Now all the council officials had not agreed with the proceedings against Jesus. But being aware of the opinion and consensus of the great majority and fearing to stand up against it, they had deliberately not attended when invited to the nighttime meeting and so did not observe the hearing. Joseph of Arimathea was in their number. He was a rich man and owned a garden quite close to the place of execution. He had sent a servant who let him know everything that happened to Jesus. When it was reported to him that Jesus was dead, he immediately requested the corpse from Pilate. Pilate consented. The Roman soldiers took the crucified one from the cross and gave him to Joseph's servants. The latter had brought cloths and various spices. Mary Magdalene anointed the body of her beloved master with myrrh, the ointment of love and joy (Song 1:2–3), and then the servants wrapped him in clean linen cloth. This done, they laid him in a new tomb (Gen. 25:9) which Joseph had had hewed out of a rock (Isa. 22:16). The aroma of myrrh, aloe, and cinnamon filled the chamber (Ps. 45:8). After the servants had rolled a heavy stone to the opening of the tomb, Mary Magdalene still remained sitting close by. Night came, and she sank crying into a sea of lamentation. No one was there to comfort her (Lam. 1:2).

Meanwhile the disciples had scattered far away. They were afraid in the city, so most of them fled in haste and immediately made their way to Galilee. Simon also had left the house of the high priest in full flight. But as he made it outside the city he heard the crowing of a rooster. The cry of the rooster woke him out of his panic and reminded him of the words Jesus had spoken to him the night before. He was overcome with shame and began to cry bitterly.

Fourth Act

Resurrected — Escaped from the Snare of the Hunter

In the middle of the night the Word arose and signs occurred which became prophetic lore and the testimony of witnesses.

> **You cleft the earth**
> **and streams broke forth....**
> **You went forth to redeem your people,**
> **to rescue your anointed one.**
> **You tore the roof from the house of the wicked**
> **and laid bare their foundation.** (Hab. 3:9, 13)

The door was removed from the tomb, and the foundations of a long human history, with its hopes and lies, with its attempts at reconciliation and deeds of murder, were laid bare (Isa. 26:21).

God spoke one thing from the midst of his mysterious darkness, and it was heard in multiple ways by the disciples in the broken light of the human day. They hastened to collect what had been scattered.

•

After the Sabbath some women hurried to the grave in the garden of Joseph of Arimathea. Their hearts were possessed by grief, and their minds were fixed on the death of their beloved master, whom they wanted to give a last sign of their devotion. When they passed by Golgotha, it seemed to them that the many stones lying about there were like a valley of bones (Ezek. 37:1–2). Since the last cry of their crucified master they saw death everywhere. At the tomb they found

the stone rolled away and they gasped (Song 5:6): the corpse was not
to be seen. Nonetheless they dared to go into the tomb chamber. Suddenly a light met them, and they were so terrified that they began
to shake. A form in white garments appeared before them and said:
"Fear not! Praise God forever (Tob. 12:17). You seek Jesus the crucified, but he is no longer here (Song 5:6). Go and say to his disciples:
'He has risen and goes before you to Galilee.'" In dread and fear they
fled from the tomb, stumbling and almost falling to the ground for
terror.

The report of the open and empty tomb shook Simon out of
his sorrow, shame, and confusion. He met another disciple, who was
likewise awakened from his gloomy dejection by the message of the
women. Together they ventured out to the tomb in the vicinity of
the city that was still dangerous for them. They found everything as
the women had reported it to them. Then Simon remembered how
Jesus had appeared in light to him, James, and John on the mountain beyond the Jordan and had spoken of being delivered over to
sinners. Just as clearly he remembered his rebuke of Jesus, because at
that time he had been unable to comprehend. Yet meanwhile much
within him had changed. The tears of the past days had drenched his
innermost being. He began to understand what he had not understood. The words of his master, which he still vividly remembered,
became like grains of mustard which began to put forth the first small
roots in the ground of his soul.

Mary Magdalene was alone and cowered before the tomb. For her
the sky was clothed in black and covered with garments of mourning
(Isa. 50:3). But then she heard, through the veil of her tears, a voice
that said, *Woman, why are you weeping?* Without looking at the one
who spoke to her she answered, "They have taken away my lord and
I don't know where they have laid him." Then she turned and saw a
form, which once more asked, *Woman, why are you weeping? Whom
do you seek?* She thought it was the gardener and, hanging on the last
visible sign of her beloved master as she sought him in the garden
(Song 6:1–2), she said, "If you have carried him away, tell me where
you have laid him so that I can get him and take him with me." With

these words she had already turned back again to the empty tomb. Then she heard from behind her, *Mary!* The voice went through her body and carried away her soul (Song 6:12). A tender power turned her to the one who spoke to her. With widened eyes she looked at him and could say only, "Rabboni [Master]!" Then she fell to the ground before him, tremblingly embraced his feet, and kissed them (Ps. 2:11). Jesus said to her, *Don't hold me tight, Mary, because for your sake I am not yet with my Father. Go to my brothers and sisters and say to them: "I am ascending to my Abba and he will also be your Father; you will be my brothers and sisters"* (2 Sam. 7:14).

What he said made her happy and pained her at the same time. She had scarcely been summoned out of the ocean of her sorrow and she already experienced his departure. Yet new life was beginning to fill her. The words that he had spoken to her freed her not only from her search for the corpse, but in the beatific "Mary!" she found him and her own self in the very depths of her soul. She turned him loose; he wiped away her tears (Isa. 25:8) and disappeared from her sight.

Meanwhile, Simon was in agony. An intimation of faith in his heart was struggling with a mind which could still understand very little. Far from other people he sought peace in lonely paths among trees and rocks. He looked up for a moment from his brooding and was startled to see a bright form in front of him whose coming he hadn't noticed. Anxiety and confusion still filled him to his bones, and now he was terrified. But immediately he heard the words, *Fear not!* The sound of the voice made him shake, and he heard it speak again, *Have trust! It is I.* Then he recognized him and, shaken, he moved back. Although everything in him was waiting for this very voice, all he could do was stammer, "Lord, go away from me, for I am a sinful man." He began to reel and the hills about him seemed to rock (2 Sam. 22:8). Even though he stood on a stony path, he had the impression he was sinking in torrents of water (Ps. 18:4). Then he heard again, *Peace be with you!* A hand reached out to him and drew him out of the torrents. Simon fell to his knees before Jesus. The Lord said to him, *Your sins are forgiven you.* The hand lifted him up, and he heard clearly, *I will make you a fisher of men. Go, gather and strengthen your brothers and sisters.* Simon was able only to stammer the name of Jesus before he was once again alone. He rushed away to tell the others.

The Slain Messiah and Light from the Scriptures

Two disciples left the city going to the west. Early in the morning they had heard from the women that the tomb was empty. But this report seemed like empty talk and didn't cheer up their downcast spirits. Although they weren't learned in the Scriptures like the scribes, they had done much reading in the holy books. They comprehended well that the Israel in distress and sinfulness did not correspond to what God intended to make of his people. So they had followed Jesus. He had stirred up a living hope in them that he would liberate the nation from evil. Yet something quite different had occurred. Had the prophet from Nazareth not become like a deceitful brook and waters that fail (Jer. 15:18)? The hope in their hearts had not been completely extinguished — but the bitter events had paralyzed them and stunned their spirit.

While they talked with each other in great dejection, a traveler overtook them whose nearness they hadn't noticed. He seemed, however, to have heard something of their conversation, for he asked them the reason for their sorrow. Astonished that he seemed to know nothing of the recent events, they began to tell him all that had happened in Jerusalem. Since he listened to them sympathetically, they opened their hearts to him and spoke of their hopes and disappointments.

Almost imperceptibly he took up their questions and began to go through the Holy Scriptures with them. He explained to them how the people on the way to liberation continually murmured against Moses (Exod. 15:24) and banded together against him (Num. 16:3). The prophets and messengers of God had to endure a similar fate. Kings, priests, and false prophets ridiculed them (2 Chron. 36:16) and tried to set traps for them (Hos. 9:8). The people sought the life of the righteous (Jer. 11:18–23) and killed them (Neh. 9:26). Then the traveler showed how, in the sacred songs of Israel, lying and violent evildoers continually conspired against David, the anointed of God, and against the worshiping community so as to take away their life. The stranger concluded by saying, *The fate of Moses, the prophets, and the anointed king shows the way the Messiah must travel to come into his glory.* Both disciples stopped and stood with open mouths, for the Scripture had never yet been interpreted to them like this. Their frozen hearts began to melt a little, and much of what they had heard earlier from Jesus began to come back to them. Since the one who walked with them understood their sorrow so well and was so knowledgeable in Scripture, they let their questions have free rein: "The scribes read the holy books differently and teach that all suffering will cease in the messianic time. If the Scripture speaks of the persecution of the prophets and the righteous, then they see in this only signs for the premessianic era. Does the Scripture actually say that also the Messiah will be persecuted?" The traveler let the Scripture speak to them. *You know, don't you, what the psalm says?*

> **The kings of the earth rise up,**
> **the rulers take counsel together**
> **against the Lord and his anointed.**
>   (Ps. 2:2)

Didn't David envision with prophetic foresight that the kings of the earth would unite against the Messiah, the anointed of the Lord, and persecute him? The two disciples had meanwhile utterly forgotten their grief and began to take up enthusiastically what the stranger was saying:

> Yes, we know that in the days of the Messiah the kings of the earth will approach with their troops for a great battle against Jerusalem. But doesn't Scripture teach that God will destroy all its foes (Zech. 12:1–9)? Doesn't he give his anointed the power to break the pagans and the godless with an iron rod (Ps. 2:9), and to burn them up with the fiery breath of his mouth (Isa. 11:4)? How can the Messiah be struck down and killed by his enemies if he is such a victorious warrior?

The traveler let the question hang between them for some time before he spoke again.

How much time has passed since Moses, David, and the prophets? Do you believe God would have waited so long if he wanted simply to destroy the evildoers? His patience endures from generation to generation (Ps. 100:5), *and his faithfulness extends to the clouds* (Ps. 36:5). *He has compassion on humankind and waits in everlasting love* (Isa. 54:8) *until the wicked and godless return* (Ezek. 18:23). *God is still the same God, even in the days of the Messiah.*

One of the two disciples broke in:

The preachers in the synagogues always preach that

Mercy is with God, but also wrath. (Sir. 5:6)

Will not the wrath of God be poured out on all transgressors of Torah in the days of the Messiah, and his mercy on the holy remnant of Israel?

The unknown visitor jumped on the word "wrath":

Yes, there is wrath. But the Holy One of Israel is God and not man (Hos. 11:9). *Because he bears with all creation in great patience, human beings can become possessed by the evil impulse of their hearts and see everything only from the standpoint of their own suffering. That is why the world becomes darkened for them and the sky over their heads becomes brass* (Deut. 28:23). *A veil is laid over the peoples and a covering over the nations* (Isa. 25:7). *Even for Israel the luminous countenance of the Lord will disappear, and it can hear his words only as stammering* (Isa. 28:13). *In their suffering the wicked torture and persecute one another until their violent deeds fall back on them* (Ps. 7:12–16). *Thus they exist under wrath. Yet God's judgment is light for the world* (Isa. 26:9).

This penetrating explanation stirred and excited both disciples. What this one walking the way with them said seemed to them oddly bright and clear, and yet they had never heard a similar interpretation of Scripture. After they had walked beside him silently for some time he began to speak again, and now he had the air of touching on a mystery.

In the days of the Messiah wrath will go throughout Israel and the entire earth. Therefore the anointed one, like Moses and David, like the prophets and many righteous, will be persecuted and rejected. However, the marvelous hand of the Lord is with him. Do you know the verse from the psalm?

**The stone that the builders rejected
has become the cornerstone.**
(Ps. 118:22)

Who in Israel could be rejected and made the cornerstone at the same time? The builders, they are the sinners in whom the wrath works and who reject the stone. The Lord, however, does not give his anointed over to the wicked. Do not the redeemed themselves affirm this?

**He reached from on high and took me,
he drew me out of violent waters.
He delivered me from mighty foes,
who hated me and were too strong for me. . . .
He brought me into a broad place;
he delivered me because he delighted in me.**
(Ps. 18:7, 10)

So King David, in prophetic foresight, has the Messiah speak: though thrown down into the abyss by his foes, he is drawn by God's hand out of the depths and exalted to the right hand of his power (Ps. 110:1–2).

The way of the Messiah moved like a great picture before the eyes of the two disciples. Their hearts came alive, and they themselves were brought into a broad place. The world had changed in and around them.

After quite some time they came out of their astonishment and reflection, and one of them posed yet another question: "Is the Messiah so weak that his enemies can cast him into the abyss?" The mysterious teacher, whom they encountered so unexpectedly on the way, said initially only, *What is weakness?* After a long silence he continued:

> *How could the Servant of God be weak, since the Spirit of the Lord rests upon him* (Isa. 42:1)? *But when his foes rise up against him, then the Spirit teaches him not to return evil with evil. In hearing God day by day he turns his back to his adversaries, offers his cheeks to the mockers and his face to those who spit on him* (Isa. 50:4–6), *and he lets himself be led like a lamb silently to the slaughter* (Isa. 53:7).

Now the hearts of the disciples began to grow fervent. Hadn't their master let himself be delivered over exactly like that? Both cried out almost simultaneously, "Then have the high priests, the elders, and the scribes committed an injustice when they condemned Jesus? In spite of the crucifixion, God has not rejected the prophet from Nazareth." Their mysterious traveling companion gave them no direct answer, but he replied only,

> *Remember in the prophet Isaiah what the sinners say about the Servant, whom they themselves struck down, after their conversion:*

> **We thought he was stricken,**
> **smitten by God and afflicted.**
> **But he was pierced for our transgressions. . . .**
> **And with his stripes we are healed.**
>
> (Isa. 53:4–5)

Human beings always say that God avenges himself with great impatience, but they actually attack one another themselves. They always say that the others are guilty, but their guilt strikes down the Servant. Only those are able to recognize the Messiah who can see their own guilt.

The eyes of the disciples lost their focus, and they began involuntarily to think about their flight when Jesus was arrested. They were overcome with deep shame, and a new unrest and anxiety formed in them. "Will God punish those who were guilty of his Messiah's suffering and death?" The stranger allowed the question to remain for a moment before responding.

No one knows the final ways of God with humankind. But have trust and remember the word of the Lord through the prophet Zechariah:

Upon the house of David and upon the inhabitants of Jerusalem I will pour out the Spirit of compassion and supplication. When they look on him they have pierced, they will mourn for him as for an only child. (Zech. 12:10)

Evening had come, and in the disciples a deep peace had lodged. Their burning hearts had lost all their anxiety.

Meanwhile they had arrived in the village of their destination. The stranger, who had become their marvelous teacher, started to depart from them, but they pressed him to lodge for the night with them. At table he took the bread, blessed and broke it. Then they recognized him. Yet before they could grasp it in their initial shock, he disappeared before their eyes. Their jubilant cries broke out: "He lives. Our hearts had already begun to burn within us as he explained the Scripture to us; only our eyes didn't recognize him." Although it had become dark outside, they set out again and returned in haste to Jerusalem. A new light led them through the night.

A Living Sign for All Peoples

Simon was on his way to Galilee. Initially he felt so light, as if he was borne by the wings of the wind (Ps. 18:10). Never before had he experienced so intensively how new life sprouted forth after the early rains. Grass was growing, flowers were bright in the cheerful colors, and even the rocky mountains drew a delicate green over themselves. Trees bore their blooms or were already putting out the first fruits (Ps. 104:14–16). The pungent aromas of coriander, mint, and rue followed his way and made him feel the new power of life. But over everything arched a sky which disappeared on the horizon like the sea and across which clouds traveled like ships.

As he wandered along he looked up at the deep blue (Job 35:5) and let his soul glide into it as into eternity. Heaven and firmament took him along with them in declaring the glory of the Lord (Ps. 19:1).

Simon was traveling by himself, but for a short stretch a man from Egypt accompanied him. The latter told him of the great stone monuments that rose up many hundreds of yards toward heaven. The ancient kings, the pharaohs, intended the massive monuments to be built over their tombs as stone memorials of them for all future generations. While the Egyptian enthusiastically recounted his narrative, trying to impress the man from Galilee, the image of the grave of Jesus came again before the eyes of Simon. It was not covered, but open and empty. In the burial chamber no corpse decayed. For the remembrance of the one crucified no dead stones were needed, for he lived in Simon's wounded and healed heart. As Simon mused on the picture of the empty tomb a word of David stole unexpectedly into his mind and came as a kind of whispering in his ear (Job 4:12):

> I have the Lord constantly before me....
> Therefore my heart is glad and my soul rejoices;
> my body also dwells secure.
> For you do not give me up to the underworld,
> or let your godly one see the pit. (Ps. 16:8–10)

What did David mean in this song? He himself had died and he, Simon, had seen his sealed grave more than once in Jerusalem. The prophetic King David could not have meant himself but must have meant another. Simon shivered at the thought that David, so many generations ago, had been able to see what had happened in Jerusalem even now. He began intuitively to understand the deeds of God into which he, the lowly fisherman from Galilee, would be taken up.

The Egyptian had meanwhile continued his narrative. Simon interrupted his long-winded description of the mighty monuments in stone: "The God of Israel will erect an altogether different monument on the border of Egypt" (Isa. 19:19–20). Then he began to tell him about Jesus and ended with how they had discovered the open and empty tomb. The Egyptian was taken aback in astonishment, and finally he exclaimed, "I have never heard anything like this." After their ways parted, Simon remained long in thought about the strange ways of God.

The Lord will reveal himself to the Egyptians, and the Egyptians will acknowledge the Lord on that day. (Isa. 19:21)

From Simon to Peter

As Simon drew near to the region at the upper end of the sea, new questions began to press upon him. Would the others believe him? Who would lead them in the future? Until now they needed only to follow in the steps of Jesus, who had gone out before them. In spite of the joy in his heart Simon felt suddenly lost, and the nearer he came to his home area the more insecure and despairing he became.

John and Jacob, the sons of thunder, were happy when he came to them. It had deeply confused, even bewildered them that Jesus had allowed himself to be taken without resistance. But by the same token, shame began to nag at them because of their flight from danger. Their rashly irascible inclination to call down fire from heaven was yielding to a readiness to listen more attentively and deeply so that they might grasp the incomprehensible. Simon recounted everything he had experienced and they asked many questions. The account of his betrayal and his tears unleashed the deeply penetrating feelings of their own shame, and they relived with horror the death of their master on the cross. They were all ears for what Simon had to say, and the words they heard stirred them without measure.

A long silence followed Simon's narrative. Finally John, still in astonishment, was able to say, "God didn't attack with fire from heaven. Nevertheless, he rescued our master from the hands of his foes. We ran away, while the earth was made to give up her dead" (Isa. 26:19).

This good news spread rapidly among the disciples in Galilee. It awoke new hopes and counteracted doubt. Simon didn't know what to do next, so after a period of waiting and perplexity he returned to his earlier work. Some of the circle of the twelve who were with him followed him. During the first night, when they again cast their nets out into the sea, they caught nothing and were worried (Isa. 19:8). In the morning, however, the sea became completely quiet, and as they slowly made their way back scarcely a sound was to be heard. They hoped silently for something to help them (Lam. 3:26). Then they saw a traveler standing on the bank, who asked if they had something to eat. When they told him no, he said, *Cast your nets out on the right side of the boat!* They followed the strange advice without knowing why, and soon they caught so many fish that they couldn't haul the nets into the boat, but had to pull them behind it. John turned suddenly to Simon: "It's the Lord!"

Simon came up out of his familiar workaday world like someone who awakened suddenly from sleep (Gen. 28:16). He hastily put on his outer garment and sprang into the water. But he didn't dare speak directly to the mysterious traveler. He helped the other disciples pull the net to shore. There they saw a fire of burning coals and a loaf of bread beside it. Jesus said to them, *Bring some of the fish that you just caught.* After everything had been prepared, he took the bread, blessed it, and gave it to them. He did likewise with the fish cooked on the coals. Although they knew who he was, no one dared ask him a question, for they were as in a dream.

After the meal he caught their glances and said to them, *You have caught fish; now you shall become fishers of men. The harvest awaiting you is great. Pray to the Lord that he may call many workers who will gather it with you!* Then he turned to Simon and surprised him by asking, *Do you love me?* Simon's heart began to beat wildly in his chest (Isa. 21:4), because he remembered his betrayal. He could only stammer, "You know, Lord, that I love you." Yet Jesus repeated the same question twice, and each time it bored deeper into his wound and his shame, until suddenly, in the depth of his soul, it reached a current of peace. Then he heard the words of Jesus: *I will make you into a rock. Therefore from now on you shall be called Peter. The key to the kingdom of heaven I place on your shoulder* (Isa. 22:22). *Gather and strengthen my brothers and sisters!* With these words Jesus disappeared from their sight.

Faith in the Name of Jesus — and Doubt

The twelve had gathered, but fear was on their faces and they had barred the doors. Together they bore everything which they had experienced and heard since the death of their master, and they were trying to understand the signs that they had been given. Thomas doubted, however, and was stiff-necked. "We had previously expected," he said, "to see him work miracles. Nevertheless, his power could not save him. Weren't we deceived then, and haven't you now seen ghosts? It's not possible for me to believe if I cannot touch him and his wounds."

They began a simple meal and remembered how they had so disgracefully deserted him after the last common meal. All of a sudden he was in the midst of them, saying, *Peace be with you!* The wounds of their shame and disappointment broke open and yet were marvelously healed at the same time. He said, *Have faith in the Father and you will understand.* Then he turned to Thomas: *Come here and touch me; don't be faithless, but believing!* The heart of the disciple shook, and he could only stammer, "My Lord!" Jesus replied, *Blessed are those who have deeper sight because they don't look with their bodily eyes.* Then he spoke to all of them: *Recognize the work of the Father! I want you to be gathered in his name; but sin pierced me and you scattered. The peace from above will lead you anew to the mountain of promise. Sanctify his name and be at one with each other — then the world will know that he has sent me.*

He vanished, and they noticed for the first time what deep peace he had bequeathed to him. The word of the prophet Ezekiel occurred unexpectedly to one of them.

When I gather the house of Israel out of all the lands among which they are scattered, then I will manifest myself in them as holy, and they will know that I, the Lord, am God. (Ezek. 28:25–26)

They spoke long about what Jesus said and the prophetic promise. Thomas was silent at first, until he suddenly agreed with what the others were saying: "In him the destiny of our people is fulfilled. As Israel in the time of Ezekiel was stricken and scattered, so the blows of his enemies struck him at Passover, and we scattered. Yet God did not abandon him and led us together again. It's not because I touched him with my own fingers that I believe; my soul felt the wound that unbelief inflicted on him."

The others were astonished by Thomas's words, and in their peace they also began to feel the wounds that unbelief caused. They thanked God and praised the name of Jesus. Their thanks and praise and great joy went out to all the brothers and sisters who followed Jesus.

After some time they came together from all directions at a mountain where they were called together after their scattering. There were about five hundred men and women. James, a blood relative of Jesus, was among them. He had not participated in the great rejection at Nazareth, but he had remained uncertain until he experienced a calling just a short time before. He said to the disciples he met, "I loved him from his early youth on, but in spite of his solidarity with the holy tradition he often seemed to me so independent. I actually tried to find out whether he was secretly proud. When we later heard what the Pharisees said about him, the tongues wagged in Nazareth, but I was afraid he had been possessed by an evil spirit. The news of his execution was for most people a final confirmation of their opinion, but he revealed himself to me. Now I know that God has had compassion on our people again."

The night was passing. Most of those assembled were in a hollow and, restless from waiting and expectation, watched and prayed part of the time but sometimes grew tired and slept. Many hoped that the new kingdom would begin now. In the early part of the next day, as the light of dawn broke (Isa. 58:8), a cry spread through the crowd, "Jesus!" They saw him on a nearby peak, covered in light as with a garment (Ps. 104:2). With the common outcry the form became clearer, and a voice as from the Most High went forth (Sir. 24:3) and made the earth gently vibrate (Prov. 8:27–30). It said to them:

From the Father in heaven I was sent, and I took root in Israel (Sir. 24:12). I rejoiced to be with human beings (Prov. 8:31). I let myself be struck down into the depths of death in order to seek the lost and to bring forth abundant fruit. You are my fruit, and you will not be alone. My word goes out with you into all the world (Ps. 19:4) and does not come back empty. It accomplishes that for which it is sent out (Isa. 55:11). Gather in everyone in my name!

The voice sounded further, but it could no longer be understood. Many shouted, "Jesus, our Messiah!" The name of the Lord had taken bodily form in him. But the figure dissolved slowly into light and vanished in the quiet of the morning, which was not disturbed by wind or rustling.

Many fell to their knees when they heard the voice; others stood there astonished, while still others were puzzled and struggled with themselves over it. A great number heard clear words, while some said only a distant sound came to their ears. Besides the eleven and many who believed in the Risen One and his incarnate name, there were others who wondered whether they had not been subject to a great deception when they saw the form in the morning light.

The Holy Spirit and the New Vineyard

In thanksgiving for the early harvest Israel celebrated the Feast of Weeks fifty days after Passover (Lev. 23:15–21), and many pilgrims traveled up to Jerusalem. The murdered shepherd, who had been awakened to new life, led also his scattered flock back to that city which had become so menacing for them. They were led without knowing what awaited them.

The eleven, the other disciples, and the women spent the evening of the holy day together in common prayer, and they thanked God for the new, mysterious life of their master. In the early morning, when it was still dark, while they praised the Lord with holy songs (Isa. 30:29), their singing suddenly broke off and their ears were opened (Isa. 50:4–5). They heard a sound far off as from the rushing of many waters (Ezek. 1:24). It was a stormwind roaring (Ezek. 1:4), while all deeply in their own souls began to sense a delicate ringing. It was like the chirping of many cicadas, like a concert of angels, which penetrated ever more deeply into their ears with their beautiful tones. The roaring from afar came nearer, swelled to a mighty whirring (Ezek. 3:13), and yet reached each person as the whisper of a secret voice (Job 4:16). It roused in all of them a tender pleasure, through which their souls and thoughts relaxed and opened up. The roaring and ringing filled the room, covered everyone, and stole their souls out of their reserve.

Out of the whirlwind came tongues of fire (Sir. 48:9). Sparks of fire, each of them different, settled down on each of them (Sir. 42:22, 24). A power filled them which straightened their distressed and bent bodies, while winged creatures with faces like eagles and lions, like oxen and humans, rose up before them (Ezek. 1:4–21). They were enraptured; they did not lose consciousness, but all the same they didn't know what was happening to them. Prophetic words came suddenly to the tongue of one disciple, and he proclaimed loudly to the gathered community:

> After that it shall come to pass
> that I will pour out my spirit on all flesh.
> Your sons and daughters will be prophets,
> your old men will dream dreams
> and your young men will see visions.
> Even upon the servants and maidservants
> will I pour out my spirit in those days.
> And I will give signs
> in heaven and on earth.... (Joel 2:28–30)

Now they began to understand. The powerful roaring that came from heaven fused with the beautiful whispering and humming in their ears and became a chorus of many voices. Their tight and closed throats opened up, releasing voices which sang a new song (Jud. 16:13) and extolled and praised God with the "Holy, holy, holy" of the seraphim (Isa. 6:3). Without their knowing how this shocking event occurred, the holy and terrifying and forbidden name "Yahweh" came to their lips as a matter of course (Isa. 44:5), and they called out to him as "Abba."

As they spoke in tongues, which were precipitated by a mysterious power within them, they entrusted themselves to the Holy Spirit that had come upon them. The bolted doors of the house were opened, and, moved by a common will, they streamed out into the street to sing the praise of the Lord to all the world. Their hearts breathed in freedom.

Public Proclamation and the New Community

Although it was still early in the morning, many Temple worshipers
were already hurrying through the narrow streets. So it was that a
considerable crowd was gathering about the group of men and women
who sang in such an odd manner and whose uplifted arms waved like
ears of corn in the wind. Many who pushed forward out of curiosity were from foreign lands, having come to Jerusalem to worship and
offer sacrifices in the Temple. They listened and were astonished, because they heard songs of praise and thanksgiving in their own mother
tongue. Some wondered whether this whole bunch had fallen into
prophetic ecstasy (1 Sam. 10:10–11). But others only laughed and
said, "These people are full of sweet wine."

Out of the circle in which the new song resounded Peter stepped
out and spoke to the gathered crowd: "Hear this, you dwellers of Jerusalem and you god-fearing Jews from the Diaspora! These men and
women are not drunk, as you may think. The day has scarcely begun. No — for now is fulfilled what the prophet Joel announced long
ago. God pours out his Spirit on the sons and daughters of Israel to
give them salvation and freedom." Someone interrupted, "Why do you
speak and sing in such a strange way?" A woman among the disciples
was then filled with the Spirit and proclaimed:

> **Then the maidens will rejoice in the dance,**
> **young and old shall be merry.**
> **I will turn their mourning into jubilation,**
> **comfort them, and give them gladness for sorrow.**
>
> (Jer. 31:13–14)

Many had recognized the words with which Jeremiah had announced the time of returning to the homeland after exile. So they
asked, "Who are you then?" Peter replied,

> Jews like you. Yet we testify to Jesus of Nazareth. God sent him
> and attested him with mighty deeds, which many of you were
> able to see and hear for yourselves. But your leaders rejected him,

and here in Jerusalem he was condemned by Israelite people, to whom we also belong, and handed over to the Romans for crucifixion. God, however, did not turn him over to the underworld, but liberated him from the depth of the sea and delivered him from the grave (Jon. 2:2–9). In him the God of our fathers has not destroyed enemy troops as in the exodus from Egypt, but has overcome the power of the underworld. So know with certainty that God has made Jesus Lord and Liberator.

The crowd was silent and astonished, for the words of Peter caught their attention and reached the hearts of many. Some asked what they should do. Peter answered, "Believe in the name of Jesus and call on him! Any who have further questions, come tomorrow and ask again" (Isa. 21:12).

While the crowd slowly dispersed, the disciples and the women with them wondered at what had happened to them. Peter could hardly grasp that he had dared to speak so freely to such a throng and that the word he spoke was placed in his mouth (Isa. 51:16). All of them felt like new men and women, and they became suddenly aware that since the encounter with Jesus they had lived under a great inner tension. He had fascinated them, but they had not grown up into what he offered them. Yet now they were freed from the pressure that his message had awakened in them. The deep anxiety about the murderous city had flown away and become transformed into the will to give witness to Jerusalem. They said to one another, "Now we're beginning to understand the message of God's rule."

But what *had* happened to them? Both disciples for whom Jesus had clarified the Scriptures on the way to Emmaus spoke up: "The words of the prophets, which we have been reading in recent weeks, speak often of the Spirit of God. We thought they referred to that Spirit of the Lord which raised Jesus from the grave and will give all the dead new life at the end of days (Ezek. 37:1–14). But now something new has come upon us which he didn't explain to us at that time." That disciple to whom the words of the prophet Joel had been given could not interpret his own proclamation. So they read

again what he had already proclaimed to them, and they were astonished to ascertain that the Spirit also came upon them. It had not only
anointed Jesus as Messiah, but made them all prophets.

Peter remembered the question of his first hearers and passed them
on to the Spirit-filled community: "What should we do with those
who want to join us?" While they deliberated, a word was granted to a
woman and she called out to all the others, "Baptize them in the name
of Jesus!" Everyone marveled that a woman instructed them. But they
agreed quickly with her word, for Jesus had let himself be baptized
by John at the beginning of his work, and already many of them had
been baptized. They decided therefore that "just as the circumcision
is the sign of belonging to Israel, so baptism will designate those who
belong to us." Then Mary Magdalene made a request: "I would also be
baptized. Whoever walks down into the water and is covered by it, is
as in a grave. Our master was buried, and for long I cried at his tomb.
I would like to share his grave through baptism in order to find him
whole again." The others did not understand this strange statement
about the grave of baptism. And they even asked themselves whether
women should be baptized, since in Israel only the men received the
sign of belonging. Yet they didn't need long to consider, for the Spirit
had come in like manner upon the daughters as well as the sons of
Israel.

The next day many of those who had heard Peter preach flocked
together at the same place. The Apostle spoke to them at length
and led them out to the pool of prayer. After a long psalm they all
climbed, men and women, down into the water; they confessed and
affirmed the name of Jesus and gave themselves to baptism. With the
subsequent prayers of praise and thanksgiving the roaring sound began
again. Some of the newly baptized were terrified at first. But it was
not a storm of judgment or fire, as John had preached with his baptizing; rather their hearts and tongues were all loosed in the powerful
wind. They praised God, each as it was given to them. Among them
were some scribes who had heard the message of Peter the day before
and felt themselves strangely touched by it. They had accompanied
the others, but had not committed themselves to be baptized be

cause they still had many questions. Nonetheless, their tongues were
also loosed in the roaring. Astonished, they said afterward, "Now we
understand the oracle of the prophet Isaiah:

> **For I will pour water on the thirsty ground**
> **and running brooks on the dry land.**
> **I will pour my Spirit upon your descendants**
> **and my blessing on your offspring.** (Isa. 44:3)

So with the water God pours out his Spirit also on us." And they too
came forward for baptism.

Among those who had arrived at faith in Jesus there were numerous pilgrims who after the festival started back to their homeland.
They bore with them the message of what they had experienced, into
the villages of Judea and Galilee and into foreign lands. However,
those who remained in Jerusalem came together daily. The Spirit was
with them, so that their number quickly increased. Other homes were
opened to them in which they could assemble. They remembered the
words and deeds of Jesus and praised the work of God. Those among
them who had possessions prepared the common meal, and all were
invited to it without distinction — poor and rich, servants and masters,
women and men. They discovered how beautiful it was when brothers
and sisters live together in harmony (Ps. 133:1).

The inhabitants of Jerusalem were astonished over the new community in which the poor, slaves, and women were like free sons and
daughters and spoke in public about Jesus. When they asked them
why they did this, they got a counterquestion:

Don't you know the words of the prophets?

> **You all shall be called priests of the Lord,**
> **and they shall speak of you as ministers of our God.**
> (Isa. 61:6)

The deaf shall hear words which are only written and the blind
will see even in the dark (Isa. 29:18).

The Power of Liberation and
the Strange Ways of the Lord

They went up to the Temple daily for prayer. At the Beautiful Gate, which gave access to the Court of Women, a paralyzed man often sat; he was carried there by his relatives so that he could beg the faithful for alms. As Peter and John came to him on their way, he asked them also for alms. They looked at him and were touched by his need. The man saw how they were affected and hung with wide eyes on them as a hope for rescue began to grow in him. They noticed his eagerness, which for their part occasioned the trust that the Spirit from on high would heal just as it had worked through Jesus. What they saw awakened in the eyes of the sick man resonated with the hope in their own hearts. Yet a dark power seemed to flow against them from the man. Nonetheless they made themselves bear up against it, doubling their trust, and words came first to the lips of Peter: "Riches of gold and silver have we none, but we will share with you the rich blessing that God gives. In the name of Jesus of Nazareth, rise and walk!" Peter took the paralytic by the hand, and the latter felt immediately a new power to his very bones. He sprang up, walking around praising and exalting God. Some who were nearby had followed everything that had happened; others recognized the man who was with Peter and John singing songs of praise as the paralyzed man who used to sit at the Beautiful Gate. An astonished agitation spread out among the people, who flocked together.

Gripped by the Spirit that had worked the healing through them, Peter and John and the disciples accompanying them went into one of the porticos in which the scribes also used to instruct their students. Peter turned to the people following and said, "Israelites, why are you so surprised? Don't stare at us as though we had done some great marvel! In the power of the Spirit Jesus of Nazareth proclaimed the new arrival of our God. He passed through the villages and cities of Galilee; he bore the needs and burdens of us all and healed many who were sick. But our leaders suspected him of being an agent of Beelzebub and had him killed. God, however, demonstrated his liberating and lifegiving power and rescued him from death." Pointing to the healed man, who meanwhile stood quietly beside him, Peter continued: "If this man, lame until just a moment ago, stands now healthy before you, know then that the lifegiving power from above has healed him. His faith in the Risen One has given him new energy and health before your very eyes."

In fact, the healed man puzzled over what Peter was saying about him, for he had previously heard little of Jesus and in his misery had for long thought no more about him. John noticed his confusion and intervened to clarify: "We saw hope in your eyes. God heard Jesus, the Risen Lord, who in turn received our prayer for you. We took your longing to be healed to the Lord." The other disciples affirmed John's words ardently, for they had joined both apostles in prayer.

Peter continued, saying,

> Brothers and sisters, I know that the leaders of our people, the villages of Galilee, and the city of Jerusalem did not recognize Jesus. Thus was fulfilled what was already long announced in the holy Scriptures through the fate of Moses and the prophets. The Messiah, our liberator, must suffer and bear our sicknesses and sins in order to enter into his realm of glory. Learn of his way! Repent in your entire way of thinking and don't be attached any longer to yourselves and your pious thoughts! Believe in the one who was slandered and rejected. Then our people will share in healing and joy.

> **Then the lame will spring like a hart,**
> **the tongue of the dumb sing for joy.**
> **Springs will break forth in the wilderness,**
> **and streams in the desert.** (Isa. 35:6)

> If you believe, our people will be granted a time of relief and revival.

With these words astonishment ran through the throng, and a breeze of power blew through the portico. Many asked the disciples what they should do. Had the hour come when Jerusalem was beginning to hear and come to the Lord in trembling to seek his goodness (Hos. 3:5)? Were the apostles able, through the power from above, to win that city which had remained closed to their master?

Meanwhile the Temple captain had been informed that a great crowd was gathering in a portico. Since he feared a riot, he intervened with his troops and had Peter and John arrested. A number of people who were still moved by the preaching became apprehensive. They left the scene as inconspicuously as possible when they saw both apostles in the hands of the Temple guard and forgot for the moment the message of Jesus.

Peter and John shook within at the thought that they were to be led before that court which had condemned Jesus, their master and Lord. They prayed in their hearts for strength to confess him as Messiah before the leaders of Israel. They both were led before some priests and members of the high council for interrogation. They acknowledged that they had encountered the paralytic and healed him in the name of Jesus. When the council authorities heard them both speak with great candor about Jesus, then they began to fear that a matter they considered disposed of would bring about new embarrassment. But since they also noted that these two were unlearned and simple people, they conferred with one another about what course to take. They persuaded themselves that by intimidation they could stifle any further talk circulating about these false prophets. Therefore they let Peter and John present their case and then forbade them, under the threat of severe punishment, to speak again publicly of Jesus and to preach in his name. Peter answered, as it was given to him in that moment, "Judge yourselves! Is it right to listen to men rather than to God?" The authorities did not know exactly what he intended by this question. They did not respond to the question, but threatened them once more and released them.

Those who believed in Jesus now met often in the portico of the Temple, and many of the people joined them; also scribes and Pharisees became believers. The new community worshiped together and read from the Holy Scriptures. Often they were grasped by the Spirit and praised and exalted God, while some spoke in tongues. Others were given prophetic gifts, and they strengthened the community when new questions and concerns came up. Those who accompanied Jesus in Galilee asked themselves why these gifts were granted to them, since their hearts had remained so hard at that time. They knew only one answer: "Thanks to the Spirit we have lost our anxiety before one another, and the desire for the chief position by which we earlier devoured each other" (Isa. 9:19–20). Some among them occupied themselves with the daily common meal, while others instructed and taught those who were new in the way of Jesus. Each served all the others. Healings and miracles occurred through some apostles, so that the entire city spoke about it. Then the hour of decision came.

Many council authorities of the Sadducees were offended in highest measure by the conduct of the new sect. Although they had no clear accusations, they ordered the apostles — who numbered twelve again after an additional selection — to be arrested and cast into prison. On the following day the high priest summoned the entire high council to pass judgment on them. But they were taken aback when their servants found the apostles to be no longer in prison, but again in the portico of the Temple, where they taught the people who gathered. The Temple captain asked the apostles to appear before the high council, because he didn't dare try to disperse that number of people with violence. The apostles followed him voluntarily.

The high priest began the hearing in severe tones: "We prohibited you from teaching in the name of Jesus. You, however, fill the whole city with hearsay about this false prophet. Do you want to instigate the people to demand vengeance for his death?" Peter answered in the name of the others: "We have no thought of vengeance. Haven't you yourselves agreed with the judgment that it is more justifiable to obey God rather than man?" The high priest asked, "What has God commanded you?" Peter proclaimed:

> The God of our fathers anointed Jesus with the Holy Spirit and attested him by mighty deeds; but you had him crucified at the hands of gentiles. He is the stone that the builders rejected and

that God made the cornerstone. You are the builders who condemned him as a blasphemer of God; but God has installed him
as Son through resurrection from the dead. We are witnesses of
his resurrection, and God has commanded us to make it known
everywhere. Don't trust in your teachings, which have misled
you into false judgment, but believe God, who has exalted the
condemned one to Son and Messiah.

One person, much agitated, objected, "God hears no condemned person." Peter cried in response, "Remember the pagan Haman, who
wanted to destroy Mordechai and all the Jews! God let it come about
that he would be hanged on those gallows which he erected for others"
(Esther 7:10). At this a tumult began, many council members crying
in wrath, "The followers of the lying prophet are deserving of death.
Like him, they despise the high council and compare it to the gentiles. We must slay the evildoers, as Pinhas did, to liberate Israel from
the plague of this sect."

While the apostles stood before the court, the community gathered
for prayer. The Spirit had granted them a deep peace, yet at the same
time they trembled at the hostile attack and prayed with David,

> **The kings of the earth rise up,**
> **the rulers ally themselves against the Lord and his anointed.**
>   (Ps. 2:2)

Suddenly it came to them that the united assault to which the
apostles and they themselves were exposed had always dominated the
history of Israel and of the world. The fate of their master flashed
before them, and they prayed:

Truly, all the rulers of the earth, the tribes of Israel, and all the
gentiles have joined with Herod and Pontius Pilate against Jesus,
your servant, and lynched him. But you have rescued him from
death, condemned their murderous judgment, and made him the
wellsprings of truth. So now give your witnesses power this day
freely to proclaim your Word, the truth for the whole world.

With this entreaty their eyes were opened and they saw how the united powers of death imprisoned human beings since the very beginning of the world.

In the meantime, in the high council the angry cry demanding condemnation of the apostles was not unanimously supported. Some of the leaders had not experienced inner peace since the execution of Jesus. When they heard the rumor of the resurrection of the one crucified, they were even more disquieted. They were especially embarrassed by the fact that scribes and Pharisees also joined the new sect, yes, even some members of the high council seemed well disposed toward it. Thus they didn't want to let themselves be drawn again too quickly into agreement to an execution. Since the twelve, who stood before them, did not radiate that sovereignty which was so provocative in the prophet from Nazareth, they found it easier to seek some expedient.

While many weighed these thoughts, a certain Gamaliel rose up, a teacher of the Law who was highly respected by the people, and who had not been in Jerusalem when Jesus was condemned. He had the apostles led out, and then said to the council authorities,

> Consider well what you will do with these people. Other leaders have appeared who had a great following. Yet they were killed and their followers then dispersed on their own. So in this case I say, take counsel, and keep away from these men. If what Jesus began is only a human work, then his adherents will accordingly be scattered in time; if it comes from God, however, you will not be able to overthrow them. Do you want to let yourselves in for a battle with God?

The speech of Gamaliel was met with approval. The high priest had the apostles flogged and severely forbade them to preach any more in the name of Jesus. Then he released them. They, on the other hand, rejoiced that they were permitted to share a little in the fate of their master.

The fellowship of the faithful felt the work of God when the apos-

tles were given back to them out of enemy hands. In spite of the
threat a deep peace filled them. A scribe who had joined them cried
out in astonishment, "How strange are the ways of God that he installed as the Son of God that very one whom our officials rejected as
a blasphemer of God!" Another agreed with him: "How strange that
the gathering into his kingdom was preceded by an assembly of per-
secutors who wanted to do away with him!" One of them reminded
the community of the word of the Lord by the prophet Isaiah:

> **Behold, I will do again strange and marvelous things with this
>   people,
> wonderful and marvelous.
> Then the wisdom of the wise shall perish
> and cleverness of the clever shall disappear. (Isa. 29:14)**

Several scribes who observed the life of the new community were
doubtful and were torn in their thinking. They saw the unanimity
and the healings in amazement and were tremendously impressed —
yet they could not understand the belief that the Messiah had already come. As some disciples spoke to the people in the Temple,
they brought up their questions:

How can you assert that the crucified man from Nazareth is the
Messiah? Have you never read in the Scriptures that a time of
peace will be inaugurated with the coming of the Messiah?

> **Of the greatness of his government and of peace there will
>   be no end.
> Upon the throne of David he rules over his kingdom;
> he establishes and upholds it with justice and righteous-
>   ness. (Isa. 9:6)**

Where today is this righteousness of which the prophet
speaks? How can a believing Jew affirm that the Prince of Peace
has already come as long as unrighteousness prevails and pagans
dwell in the land?

The Pharisees observed that the disciples appeared uncertain and so continued with fervor:

Wickedness spreads out everywhere. But the prophet says about the time of the Messiah,

> **They shall not hurt or destroy in all my holy mountain;**
> **for the land shall be full of the knowledge of the Lord**
> **as the waters cover the sea. (Isa. 11:9)**

Today many among the people still lack knowledge of the Torah, and the land is by no means full of the knowledge of the Lord.

The scribes glanced timidly around them in case any Romans were near, and then they pointed over to Fort Antonia and launched in again:

If the lawless gentiles even occupy the Temple mount, then could the messianic time yet have arrived? The prophet Micah says,

> **For instruction shall go forth from Zion,**
> **and the word of the Lord from Jerusalem.**
> **He shall judge between many peoples**
> **and reprove strong nations afar off.**
> **Then they shall beat their swords into plowshares**
> **and their spears into pruning hooks. (Mic. 4:2–3)**

May God grant that this time come soon, when the mighty nations of the gentiles will be judged and governed by God. But who can be so presumptuous as to assert that it is already here — in this dismal present?

The disciples had become ever more uncertain during this discourse of the scribes, which gave free rein to their inner agitation. They left without giving an answer, and they brought the question before the apostles and the community. One person said, "Jesus has entered into the glory of the Father and there rules forever in peace and righteousness." A Pharisee who had become a believer responded, "However, the Scripture says that in the messianic age the land will give its grain in abundance (Ps. 72:16) and everyone will sit without fear under his vine and under his fig tree (Mic. 4:4). But that refers to a kingdom on earth. Jesus our Messiah will surely return soon from heaven to rule from Jerusalem over all nations." Thomas was more cautious in giving his opinion: "If Israel had heeded the message of our master and if we had believed with our whole hearts, then the kingdom of God would have already come." Peter added, "If the people believed now in the name of Jesus, it would be given a season of relief and revival."

A long silence followed these words, until a woman cried out in prophetic voice, "The kingdom of God is like a grain of mustard which is cast upon the ground." John took up the prophetic word and explained:

> The ways of God are different from the ways of human beings. His peace and his righteousness do not spread out by destroying the evildoers and godless with fire from heaven. Our master let himself be pierced by evil, and he transformed it through his love. Therefore the time of Messiah could come even if strife and unrighteousness continue to prevail in the world. The kingdom of God is like a grain of mustard which is sown in soil with many weeds. It slowly grows and expands everywhere, and only at the end of days will God separate the wheat from the weeds.

What John said strengthened and encouraged the community and they experienced peace once more. They marveled at the mysterious ways of God and gave thanks for the knowledge that was granted to them.

The Embodied Remembrance

The number of those who believed in Jesus grew further. When the community had assembled at mealtime, someone from the Greek Diaspora spoke with a prophetic voice: "If we live in peace and righteousness, Jesus the Messiah is present with us." These words evoked a response in everyone, and a new feeling of being the messianic community grew among them — a community in which the Prince of Peace already ruled but a community located amid quarrelsome and warlike peoples. Again a prophetic word came into the increased expectation: "We are the body of Jesus, the body of the Messiah." They had never heard a message such as this. Many were astonished; others were uncertain. Had a lying spirit suddenly crept in?

The apostles met with the disciples who were well versed in Scripture and could give counsel on the prophetic words. The message of the body of the Lord reminded the twelve of the last meal with their master and the words he had spoken over the bread and wine. They had to affirm to their own surprise that they hadn't hitherto concerned themselves with them. He had given up his life and at the same time he designated the bread he gave them as his body. They sought a deeper understanding in Scripture, but they did not find a passage anywhere which could shed further light. But on the other hand it came to them that he had appeared to them at a meal after his death. In the middle of this initial bewilderment Andrew spoke up: "Think of what we were given to experience when the Spirit came down upon us. We praised and adored God as with one tongue and one body." Peter added with great feeling, "Yes, when we were able to heal it always seemed to me as if the trust of the sick person would merge with my faith in Jesus." What Peter said had such a deep effect on all those assembled that they began to praise God with one voice and one body.

John said, "When he was arrested we ran away, but he didn't desert us. He has taken us with him." Mary, the mother of Jesus, was with the apostles and disciples as they spoke. She was mostly quiet, yet this time she added to what John said: "Whatever happened to him, he always changed it with his heart. His body was pierced by hostile hands; nonetheless he has made himself into a food for us and for many." A long silence followed these brief words. She had carried the body of which she spoke in her own body, and she had gone with her son all the way to the cross. The silence was first broken when Mary Magdalene suddenly cried, "If the bread of blessing is his body, then it is given to us to receive him with mouth and heart." No one among them had thought in this way about Christ's body. The apostles and prophets decided that in the future they would always remember the last supper with Jesus in their daily meal.

Sin in the Community and Transformation of Evil

Some of those who possessed goods sold everything in order to give the proceeds to the community. A man named Ananias did as the others and sold in his case a piece of land. He did it in such a way that it appeared he was placing the entire sum at the feet of the apostles. With the knowledge of his wife, however, he held back a portion of the money. But Peter saw through him and asked, "Why didn't you act in freedom, but instead only imitated the others? You could have kept your land or done what you wanted with the proceeds. But you have given Satan a place in your heart and wish to deceive the Holy Spirit and the community." As Peter said this a deadly terror ran through Ananias's body. He fell to the ground and died immediately. Some young men carried him out to bury him. After a while his wife came; she didn't know what had happened. Peter asked her about the price for which they had sold the land. The wife lied like her husband. Then Peter said, "Why have you decided together to put the Holy Spirit to the test? Hark, the feet of those who buried your husband are at the door." Then she too fell dead for terror to the ground, and the young men buried her beside her husband.

A deep shudder of fear ran through the whole church. It had seen itself according to the image of the messianic time but now had to acknowledge that sin was also at work in its midst. Some wanted to comfort themselves with the thought that both evildoers had died unexpectedly and had been rooted out of the community by God himself. Yet others disagreed, saying, "Why would God destroy the sinners among us when he does not do that in Israel and in the world?" Frightened by these events, they suddenly saw sin in other aspects of their common life. There was tension among them. Those who came from the Greek Diaspora distrusted the believers from Jerusalem concerning distribution of food. Many disputes sprang up over observance of the Law. Some who had committed themselves zealously were soon lukewarm again and without evident reason stayed away from the daily gatherings.

Because of this disenchantment a frost set in on the still young and blooming hopes of many. The apostles bore the cares of all and tried to encourage them. They remembered how faint-heartedly they themselves had followed their master in Galilee and how they had even betrayed him in Jerusalem. They taught that "the weeds grow among the grain. The messianic community must live in a world of dissension and sin, and these dark powers have an effect also on the community."

This teaching did not please some of the young men and women, who were still full of unbroken zeal. They said, "We are the messianic community, the saints of the Most High (Dan. 7:18). Jesus didn't marry. We should follow him in that; then we will be a fellowship of the completely pure. He will soon return to us from heaven and we will live with him like angels and rule in his kingdom." These words disturbed the apostles deeply. They sympathized with the holy zeal of the young people, but they also detected the secret effort to exalt themselves in pride. Peter responded with a humility which touched everyone: "To whom it is given, that one should imitate our master in every respect. But it is not given to all. He was often in my house; he saw my wife and children and never reprimanded me on their account." A Pharisee who had joined them added after a while, "In the Song of Songs the Scripture also praises the love between husband and wife." One of the zealous youths objected: "But that is only an image for the love between God and his people." The Pharisee, however, asked in modest tones, "What does Solomon teach?"

Rejoice in the wife of your youth,
a lovely hind, a graceful doe!
Let her affection delight you at all times,
be enchanted always with her love.

(Prov. 5:18–19)

The young zealots fell silent in embarrassment, for they had never paid attention to these words of Scripture. Nonetheless they remained with their question: "How can we be the people of the Messiah and the saints of the Most High if we are not completely pure?" Thomas gave them this to consider: "When we were together with our master he always walked before us, and he went alone into death as we abandoned him. Likewise now he goes out ahead of the community through the Spirit he has granted us. We are not made clean through our deeds, but through him and the Spirit."

The zealots asked, "Doesn't his Spirit make us holy also?" A scribe who had come to faith in Jesus got involved in the discussion: "God chose and cleansed Israel, but in spite of that it became a harlot (Ezek. 16). Shouldn't we understand our community in light of what befell the entire people?" The zealots insisted, "But Jesus proclaimed the new coming of our God, and he wanted to free the people from all evil that earlier burdened it. Yes, Israel was a harlot until his days and so it also rejected and killed him. But we no longer belong to this unfaithful and adulterous people."

At this point Peter stepped forward and tried with faltering words to explain something he could grasp himself only with difficulty: "Yes, our master wanted to free Israel from all evil. We have followed him and we hoped for a great liberation. Nevertheless, there is much we haven't understood. Once he even turned me away from him as a tempter. Isn't there a mystery about evil? Can it not be entangled with the good? I was full of good will and wanted to help him, but he addressed me as 'Satan.' I will never forget that moment."

These words deeply affected everyone, for Peter's pain had been newly awakened and reached out to all the others. They suddenly felt how easily evil could slip in among them. Some of them became embarrassed and confused, and all of them felt the difficulty of the moment. They had come to faith in Jesus because they saw him as the Messiah and the victor over evil. And now? Someone spoke out of his distress: "How can we believe in the Messiah if not only in the world but also among us good and evil are mixed together?" There was a puzzled silence. Then John spoke: "When we drew near to Jerusalem with our master I thought God would surely destroy all the wicked with fire from heaven. Yet how I was deceived about myself! How unfaithful I was to our master! If God had destroyed all the wicked, should he not also have burned me?" The honesty of these words made everyone tremble, but they also increased the bewilderment of many. Pausing for a moment, John then continued: "By my own denial I've learned that God's ways are other than our human plans. Jesus was led by his Father from day to day and hour to hour. He could separate the good from the evil, but we groped about in the dark." Someone interrupted: "Must we always grope in the dark? Haven't we received his Spirit?"

Before one of the apostles or disciples had a chance to answer, a woman began to speak in tongues and quoted a Scripture verse to the congregation:

Go, take a prostitute as your wife. (Hos. 1:2)

Most were disturbed by this word from the prophet Hosea and wanted to disregard it. John, however, took up the woman's offering to the community and spoke:

When our master was taken prisoner we were unfaithful like harlots and ran away from him. But he bore us in his suffering as a shepherd carries a lost sheep. Did he not likewise enter into a covenant with us unfaithful ones, just as the prophet Hosea took a prostitute to wife by the command of God?

Andrew took the open question further:

At our last meal he gave us his own body to eat. In the food of the meal he became completely one with us. How heartfelt and deep the covenant he made with us and many others, that it was made through this sign of bread and wine that he shared with us.

The uneasiness and bewilderment had left the community again. The worries about their own mistakes and sins diminished, and everyone came to a new trust in Jesus. They believed in him as the Lord and the bridegroom of their fellowship. With new ears they heard what God had spoken through the prophet Jeremiah:

> **I have loved you with an everlasting love,**
> **therefore I have continued my faithfulness to you.**
> **Again I will build you**
> **and you shall be built, O virgin Israel!**
> **Again you shall adorn yourself with timbrels**
> **and go forth in the dance of the joyful.** (Jer. 31:3–4)

They had encountered the love and faithfulness of God on earth in the love of Jesus, who had offered himself for Israel and all the peoples. Also the zealots began to understand that they could not become the messianic community through their own purity; the cleansing water of the Spirit washed their sins away (Ezek. 36:25–26), and the bridegroom gave his bride both joy and adornments. She lived out of him and in his body.

Out of the silly dove, easily led astray (Hos. 7:11), emerged a dove with silver wings (Ps. 68:14), the unique, the flawless one (Song 6:9). The net that was cast over Israel when it ran in adulterous lust after Egypt (Hos. 7:12), was changed into a net for the great catch of fish, and the deeds that accusingly encompassed the community (Hos. 7:2) turned into praise of the goodness of the God whose heart recoils and changes from fierce anger to compassion (Hos. 11:9). The church sowed under persecution and reaped in peace (Hos. 8:7).

Peter gathered all who believed in the Lord Jesus and reminded them again of their perplexity.

We are wandering in the dark, in hope and not by sight, but each of us will be given a light. If we bring all the lights together, then a great clarity will enlighten us. The name of the Lord grows in strength from all the gifts together. He is the key to the kingdom of heaven.

Someone asked timidly, "And Ananias and his wife? Did Satan capture them?" The question touched on a wound. There was no response until an even darker question was posed, one which no one had dared to ask until now: "What happened to Judas? Did he also fall into the clutches of Satan?" Now John spoke up: "Our master declared a severe judgment against sin, but he himself was brought before a court of judgment." Added a former member of the council, who was now with them after having become a member of the church: "We condemned him as a blasphemer of God." Some women said, "We heard that on the cross he cried out that God had abandoned him." John concluded, "Yes, he himself shared the fate of those placed under the curse, and he went after the lost even into the darkest night."

And the congregation, already stunned by the message of the Lord Jesus they were just beginning to understand, was further astonished to hear John say: "God does not destroy the wicked and godless with fire and sword from heaven. He transforms what is evil, as we know from our own experience, and he changes it into love."

Raymund Schwager, S.J., is Professor of Dogmatics and Ecumenical Theology at the University of Innsbruck in Austria. One of his many books has previously appeared in English translation: *Must There Be Scapegoats? Violence and Redemption in the Bible.* His book *Jesus im Heilsdrama,* which is a scholarly theological companion to *Jesus of Nazareth,* will be published in English as *Jesus in the Drama of Salvation.*

James G. Williams teaches Bible and Girardian studies at Syracuse University. The executive secretary of the Colloquium on Violence and Religion, he is the author of *The Bible, Violence, and the Sacred* and the editor of *The Girard Reader.*

Of Related Interest

James G. Williams, Editor
The Girard Reader
Among the theories and principles that undergird Raymund Schwager's
book are those of philosopher René Girard, "whose work suggests the
projects of those nineteenth-century giants — Hegel, Marx, Nietzche,
Freud — who still cast such long shadows today."
— *Comparative Literature*
0-8245-1634-6; $19.95

Gil Bailie
Violence Unveiled
Humanity at the Crossroad
This visionary look at the evolution of thought on violence and
sacrifice — from the Bible, literature, and current events — reveals that
the life and death of Jesus has tremendous meaning at this turning point
in human history. Winner of the 1996 Pax Christi Award.
0-8245-1464-5; $17.95

James Alison
Raising Abel
A theological exploration of a huge change of mind: the change which
the apostles underwent as a result of Jesus' resurrection — and how that
paradigm can transform the world. "A smashing book, as profound as
theology can be." — Robert J. Daley, S.J.
0-8245-1565-X; $19.95

Please support your local bookstore, or call 1-800-395-0690.
For a free catalog, please write us at
THE CROSSROAD PUBLISHING COMPANY
370 LEXINGTON AVENUE, NEW YORK, NY 10017

We hope you enjoyed Jesus of Nazareth. *Thank you for reading it.*

crossroad